THE HOUSEWIFE'S GUIDE

TO

FRUGAL FOOD

EAT FOR $10.00 PER WEEK

By Bethany Bontrager

Dedication & Thanks

I would like to dedicate this book to my mom, who taught me
how to be frugal.

I would also like to thank my husband for his patience as I've cut
corners and pinched pennies, sometimes with not-so-tasty
results. And lastly, I'd like to thank the friends and family,
acquaintances and complete strangers who unknowingly
provided the stories and examples I've used in this book.

Contents

What Would You Do with $500?

What could you do with an extra $500.00 every month? Perhaps you are paying off debt, saving for a goal, or just looking for a way to make ends meet with a lower income.

Consider the fact that the average American household spends about $150.00 per week on food[1] (and only 8% spend less than $50.00 per week).   If you can spend only $20.00 per week on groceries, it will make you $130.00 per week richer than most. Using the tips and strategies in this book will save the frugal housewife over $6,700.00 per year- the savings will be even higher for those who have children at home. That's a lot of money.

Living Below Your Means Can be Difficult

The problem with food is that most people spend the same amount on it, regardless of family income. According to the Gallup poll referenced earlier, families making $30,000-$75,000 were spending $144.00 per week on food. For the person making $75,000, that number is only 10% of their annual income. But for the family earning $30,000, food spending adds up to a whopping 25% of household income.

[1] http://www.gallup.com/poll/156416/americans-spend-

151-week-food-high-income-180.aspx

For the lower income family, the remaining $1875.00 per month has to pay for rent, transportation, insurance and more. And it's not just low income households that have a challenge! Larger families will have to make their household income stretch farther than couples or families with one or two kids, living on the same income. No wonder it is so hard to escape the cycle of poverty or get out of debt.

The good news is that EVERYONE, whether they make a lot of money or a little, can learn to spend only $10.00 (or less!) per person, per week on groceries. That extra $500.00 or more per month can really make a difference, whatever your financial means or goals are.

What could YOUR family do with an extra $500.00 per month?

Three Types of Frugal

A while back I received an email from one of my blog readers.

"I need to figure out how to squeeze my wallet enough to feed 24 hungry campers for a day. I am on for Tuesday, and the suggested meal is burgers and hotdogs. Very simple, classic camping meal with easy prep! I sat down and started calculating cost, though, and I'm finding it's not as cheap as I thought. By the time you count in buns, condiments and sides, it all adds up. I estimated it costing around $74 for the meal. That's $3/person. And I didn't even figure in paper products. And that's also not counting the fruit/veggie/snack lunch I'm providing.

I'm not quite sure what to do. Perhaps you have some suggestions? How can I feed everyone without using up my whole month's food budget in one day?

Thank you in advance,
Happy Camper Wanna-be"

Most people, Happy Camper included, are looking for a quick and easy way to save an impossible amount of money with the skills and knowledge <u>that they already have</u>. Why is it impossible? Because deals can only get you so far. Making everything from scratch can only go so far. And menu planning can only go so far.

Which Type of Frugal Are You?

Most housewives fall under one of three categories; the Shopper, the Cook, or the Planner. Some are a mixture of the three.

The Shopper: This is the gal that knows all of the deals at all of the stores. She is the coupon queen, and has a stockpile of nearly-free canned goods and laundry soap at home. She thinks the answer to frugal food is, of course, learning how to be a better shopper.

A Shopper's weaknesses include 1) buying things that are much cheaper to make at home, 2) buying things that she will never use, 3) buying food items that go bad before she can use them, and 4) dependence on deals to cover a lack of planning. The essence of saving money is that you DON'T buy stuff, which is a concept that the Shopper finds hard to grasp.

The Cook: This is the girl who takes kitchen DIY to the extreme. When she makes a sandwich, it's on homemade bread with homemade mayo and mustard from mustard seeds that she grew herself. The meat is home-smoked and sliced deli meat, and the cheese is, of course, homemade as well.

A Cook's weaknesses include 1) making things from scratch even though they are cheaper to buy, 2) spending too much time cooking, 3) lack of attention to sales and deals, 4) making foods that go bad before she can use them, and 5) having no plan for meals. A Cook runs into trouble when she runs out of time.

The Planner: This lady thinks that proper planning is everything. She's the menu-planning guru. Not a snack is consumed without her knowing, and she knows the cost of each carrot stick eaten. Everything goes according to plan.

A Planner's weaknesses include 1) lack of flexibility in cooking, 2) lack of flexibility in shopping.

Lack of flexibility is a problem with ALL pre-made meal plans or services. They are not custom tailored to your family. One menu planning service I read about boasted of having 2,000 meals to choose from. That is great, but no automated service can juggle local deals, in-season ingredients AND your family preferences, which is essential if you are trying to live on a shoestring budget. Nobody knows your circumstances better than you do.

Menu planning is a great start to avoiding big budget-busters like restaurants, but as with DIYing or sales, it is only a piece of the puzzle. I prefer to use a meal plan template (for example, stir fry on Monday or soup on Tuesday) that can be customized on the day you cook it. This provides structure, but also gives a lot of flexibility to weekly meal planning. You can read more about this in Part 3: Planning.

How DO You Feed 24 People on a Budget?

What was holding Happy Camper back from reaching her goal? After a little back-and-forth between us, I discovered a few things.

1. Unwillingness to shop at certain places.
2. Lack of flexibility because of health standards.
3. The belief that homemade is always cheaper.
4. Lack of planning the year prior (no pantry of inexpensive/free food to draw from).
5. Brand loyalty.

The underlying problem here is NOT that feeding 24 people for less than $3.00 each is impossible. It is *entirely* possible. But when she sent her letter, my reader had the attitude that she was <u>already</u> being smart with her money, and needed confirmation of that from me. There's nothing wrong with a little affirmation, but in order to move forward, you can't be stubborn about adapting and changing your strategy... or even your priorities. Eating for $10.00 per week- or feeding a ton of hungry campers on a tiny budget- is only possible if you are willing to take advice and learn from others.

Chances are, if you are reading this book, you think you are already smart with money as well. You are doing the best you can *under the circumstances*. And you probably are. I get it- I used to be the self-righteous Cook who knew how to make mayonnaise but thought coupons were dumb. I would have rather made mustard for $5.00 per quart (DIY snobbery at its finest) than use a coupon to get it for $0.50. Like Happy Camper, I had skills, but I also had blind spots. We need Shoppers, Cooks, AND Planners to help get rid of those blind spots, so we can be the best and most frugal versions of ourselves that we can be.

In order to *really* make progress cutting the food budget, we need to learn from each other instead of making excuses like "Coupon users are hoarders" or "meal plans never work anyway" or "I don't have time to cook" or "I'm too healthy to buy food on sale... I need to make everything from scratch."

As we move forward, I beg of you to read this book with an open mind. It takes ALL skills of ALL types to live on a bare-bones food budget. And it's not lack of shopping, cooking or planning that will hold you back: it's ego and pride.

The Beginner's Grocery Budget

By utilizing the techniques in this book, you will eventually be able to eat for $5.00-$10.00 per person, per week. If you are just beginning, though, budget for $20.00 per person, per week.

Before you start stocking the pantry, the first step is to follow a weekly budget. If you have never budgeted for groceries before, I would recommend using the envelope system. First, designate two envelopes as "Bulk Buying Fund" and "Cooking Tools Fund". Then, make one envelope for each week of the month. Deposit $20.00 per person into each weekly envelope, and leave the two snowball fund envelopes empty. Allocate your weekly grocery money in the following ways:

Percentages at $20.00 per person:

Food Group	%	1 Person	2 People	3 People	5 People	8 people
Total Spending:		$ 20.00	$ 40.00	$ 60.00	$ 100.00	$ 160.00
Meat & Eggs:	30%	$ 6.00	$ 12.00	$ 18.00	$ 30.00	$ 48.00
Dairy:	15%	$ 3.00	$ 6.00	$ 9.00	$ 15.00	$ 24.00
Grains & Beans:	15%	$ 3.00	$ 6.00	$ 9.00	$ 15.00	$ 24.00
Bread:	5%	$ 1.00	$ 2.00	$ 3.00	$ 5.00	$ 8.00
Produce:	30%	$ 6.00	$ 12.00	$ 18.00	$ 30.00	$ 48.00
Miscellaneous:	5%	$ 1.00	$ 2.00	$ 3.00	$ 5.00	$ 8.00

Before you leave for the grocery store, make a list of the things you want to purchase. Remember- money will be tight, so you must plan carefully. Here is an example of what $20.00 will buy:

     1 dozen medium eggs ($1.50)

     2-3 lbs. of meat ($2.00-$3.00/lb.)

     1 gallon of milk ($3.00)

     1 lb. rice ($1.00)

     1 lb. beans ($1.00)

     1 loaf of bread ($1.00)

     1 12 oz. can tomato paste ($1.00)

     1 bag frozen vegetables ($1.75)

     2 heads cabbage ($0.80)

     2 lb. bag carrots ($1.50)

     1 5 lb. bag potatoes ($2.50)

     4 bananas ($0.80)

Amounts for Families

Food	Amount	1 Person	2	3	5	8	12
Eggs	doz.	1	2	3	5	8	12
Meat	lb.	3	6	9	15	24	36
Milk	gal.	1	2	3	5	8	12
Rice	lb.	1	2	3	5	8	12
Beans	lb.	1	2	3	5	8	12
Bread	loaf	1	2	3	5	8	12
Tomato paste	12 oz. can	1	2	3	5	8	12
Frozen veg.	bag	1	2	3	5	8	12
Cabbage	head	2	4	6	10	16	24
Carrots	lb.	2	4	6	10	16	24
Potatoes	lb.	5	10	15	25	40	60
Bananas	lb.	1	2	3	5	8	12

The prices I'm using are from Walmart, off-brand items. You will not be able to afford to buy name brand food from here on out, unless it is under special circumstances. When you are done shopping for the week, put any extra money in the "Bulk Shopping Fund" envelope or the "Cooking Tools Fund" envelope. You will read about these envelopes later.

For the first week, meals will probably look a little bleak. You will be eating a lot of meatless meals, soups, quiche, etc. At the end of this book, I've included some frugal meal ideas that you can make during the first few weeks of budgeting. Beginners should look through weekly ads to find cheap produce or cuts of meat. Milk or eggs may also be on sale. Remember, the shopping list above is just a guideline. You can make up your own percentages and buy whatever food items you want to, as long as you stay within the $20.00 per person, per week budget.

After you have worked through some of the exercises in this book- for example, six to 12 months of bulk buying- and learned to make some things from scratch (yogurt, cheese, bread, etc.), you will be able to buy a lot of food for $20.00. You will soon find out that $20.00 per person per week is too much! As you can, slowly cut the monthly family grocery budget.

Here is what your budget may look like once you have cut it down to $10.00 per person, per week. I know many large families that have probably already achieved this, so it is very doable.

Percentages at $10.00 per person:

Food Group	%	1 Person	2 People	3 People	5 People	8 people
Total Spending:		$ 10.00	$ 20.00	$ 30.00	$ 50.00	$ 80.00
Meat & Eggs:	30%	$ 3.00	$ 6.00	$ 9.00	$ 15.00	$ 24.00
Dairy:	15%	$ 1.50	$ 3.00	$ 4.50	$ 7.50	$ 12.00
Grains & Beans:	15%	$ 1.50	$ 3.00	$ 4.50	$ 7.50	$ 12.00
Bread:	5%	$ 0.50	$ 1.00	$ 1.50	$ 2.50	$ 4.00
Produce:	30%	$ 3.00	$ 6.00	$ 9.00	$ 15.00	$ 24.00
Miscellaneous:	5%	$ 0.50	$ 1.00	$ 1.50	$ 2.50	$ 4.00

Bethany's Grocery Budget

At our house, I am cooking for two people. Our budget percentages look a little different because I've learned how to exploit the resources I have available (garden space, for example) and get a lot of things for free. After a few years using the methods outlined in this book, this is what our weekly budget has evolved into:

Food Group	%	2 People
Total Spending:		$ 20.00
Meat & Eggs:	5%	$ 1.00
Dairy:	10%	$ 2.00
Grains & Beans:	10%	$ 2.00
Bread:	7%	$ 1.40
Produce:	18%	$ 3.60
Miscellaneous:	64%	$ 12.80

Our weekly shopping trip (sometimes bi-weekly...) is going into Walmart to buy one package of flour tortillas, a small container of yogurt, a 16 oz. tub of sour cream, and $5.00-$13.00 of whatever else we feel like buying (ice cream, ketchup, bargain bin items, etc.). Many of the miscellaneous items are not _needs_. If we were to run on hard times, I believe the $10.00 per person budget could be cut significantly without a hitch.

On a monthly basis, we buy carrots, onions and potatoes. Every few months I go to a discount "bent 'n' dent" store to buy pantry items (pasta, canned goods, baking items, junk food), and once or twice a year we usually buy cheese (for the freezer), rice and beans in very large quantities. As I mentioned before, fruits, veggies, meat, eggs and milk are produced on our homestead. Homesteading is not free, but I sell enough animals and food products to cover the cost of feed, vet bills, etc. I will talk about this more in later chapters.

Disclaimer: Most of this book is based on _my own experience_. Some of you may have higher or lower costs of living, access to different stores, or different skills than I have. That is okay! Regardless of who you are or where you live, I am sure there is something each one of us can do to spend less on groceries.

Eating for $10.00 per week is kind of extreme, and there are extreme methods outlined for saving in this book. As I wrote some of the sections- especially the ones about shopping at Walmart and not buying health food- I started worrying that some of my readers would hate me and not finish the book. I was afraid that people would accuse me of being immoral for putting money before health or supporting companies whose ethics I don't agree with 100%. But is it really ethical to buy expensive foods when you owe someone else that money? Is it ethical to shop at higher priced "moral" stores while you can't afford to live up to your own morals? Some of you will think it is wrong to feed children weeds or expired non-perishable food. Everyone is entitled to their own opinion, but I feel it is my responsibility to give ALL of the options when it comes to being frugal. Use your own judgement and always do what you think is appropriate when you are shopping and cooking. I am also not a professional in any area, and am not responsible if you hurt yourself or ingest something that disagrees with you.

With that out of the way, let's start saving!

Part 1: A Pantry Mindset

This chapter is for the Shoppers; the deal-sniffers, bargain-hunters, coupon-clipping grocery cart queens. You are the scavenging, sale-scouting, dumpster-diving, free box-digging and foraging masters of accumulation. And that is exactly what we need to start saving big money.

Setting Up a Pantry

Having a pantry is like having your own grocery store where all of the goods are half price, or even free. Those of you who like curb-diving and thrift store shopping will LOVE setting up a pantry, because it is all about finding great deals.

Some homes are built with a pantry already in near proximity to the kitchen. Most likely this pantry is a large walk-in closet with shelves. That is a good start, but there are a few more elements that our large scale pantry needs to have room for.

1. **A chest freezer** or two (depending on the size of your family). This will take up a lot of space and probably won't fit in a closet. But a freezer is essential if you want to save money on meat or produce. Chest freezers are more energy efficient than upright freezers, although I think food is less likely to get lost in an upright freezer.

2. **Room for five-gallon buckets.** In our pantry, my buckets of rice and beans fit perfectly on the floor underneath the bottom shelf.

3. **Shelf space for canned goods** and miscellaneous dry goods. The canned goods shelves should be at least the height of a quart-size mason jar, plus one inch on top of that (about 8 inches high). To store smaller pint or half-pint jars, you can build a shelf insert that is 4-5" high. My husband built me several of these

inserts, and now there is less wasted space in my pantry. You should also have a shelf big enough for one-gallon jars, dressing bottles, wine bottles or other taller items.

4. Lastly, **put a few hooks** inside your pantry in order to hang things on the wall. I made my rack out of a piano part. I use it to hang several grocery bags full of canning rings, my aprons, and other things.

If you don't have a designated pantry area available, consider turning your garage or basement into a pantry. Of course, you want it to be as close to the kitchen as possible. If you don't have a basement or a garage (we don't), you can also utilize other storage spaces like unused closets or the space beneath your bed. When I ran out of room in the pantry, I decided to store some of my canned meat and beans in the sewing room. The jars are in a box on the shelf, so it just looks like another box of fabric or Christmas decorations.

Sample Pantry List

Here are some things that I include on my pantry list.

Fruit: Canned peaches or pears, applesauce, strawberry jam, dried apples, dried cranberries, other dried fruits.

Vegetables: frozen sweet corn, frozen beans, frozen bell peppers, onions, garlic, potatoes, carrots.

Baking: flour, sugar, yeast, baking powder, baking soda, salt, gelatin (preferably bulk gelatin powder, but the flavored boxes are okay, too).

Beans & Grains: navy beans, pinto beans, black beans, split peas, lentils, rice, pasta.

Meats: ground meat (any kind), steaks (any kind), ham, bacon, chicken legs/cuts, roasts (any kind). I am not very picky about what kind of meat we eat. In the past year we've eaten beef, chicken, venison, goat, lamb, and pork. During our first year of marriage, my husband and I ate mostly chicken and venison.

To be honest, a lot of our meat is free or mostly free. But I do make a point to keep ham, bacon, or sausage in stock regularly because of the flavor they add to soups, casseroles, pizza or almost anything else you can think of.

In addition to what I have listed, my pantry often includes a mix of free food or things I have found steeply discounted that might not be on my "list" to buy. However, sometimes it can be a challenge to use random items because they are not on your weekly menu, and they begin to pile up. If this starts happening to you, pick one or two items every week to use up, and don't buy any more new random foods until you have used up most of your old ones.

Making a Price Book

In order to stock your pantry with food items at their lowest possible price, you are going to have to start a price book.

Each page of the book will be titled with a certain item- for example, "Oatmeal". Each time you buy oatmeal, you will write down the date, where you got the item, how much it cost, what size it was and how much it cost per unit- say, per pound or per ounce.

|

Brand/item	Store	Date bought	Total price	Size	Unit price

You can download printable price book pages at my website (www.therenaissancehousewife.com) on the "Printables and Downloads" page.

When you get back from shopping, take out your price book and receipts from every store you went to. Make an entry in your book for each item you bought. If you are buying something for the first time (and you think it will be a repeat purchase), make a new page in your price book for it.

Tip: One of my readers mentioned that she uses a price book app ("My Rock-Bottom Prices") on her phone. This way she doesn't have to carry around or keep track of paper lists. I think this is a super idea for tech-savvy shoppers.

After keeping a price book for a few months, you will know where you can buy each item consistently for the cheapest price. After a year, you will also know WHEN to buy certain items. For example, you'll see that different fruits and veggies go on sale during certain months. You'll notice that ham and turkey go on sale during the holidays. Perhaps you'll realize that peanut butter or eggs or cream cheese consistently go on sale every three months. Knowing when the sales run will allow you to predict how MUCH to buy. That way the item will take up less room in your pantry or freezer.

Tip: At the time of this writing, our family includes only my husband and I. Food lasts a long time for us, so instead of making a page for every single food item, I make a page for each category (for example, "Beans") and leave five or six spaces between individual items. I'm only going to buy beans a few times a year, so to have a whole page for each *type* of bean would be overkill.

Using the information you've gathered in the price book, make a condensed version that you can take shopping with you- a price *list*.

Making a Price List

The price list is similar to a price book, but it is a condensed version that you can print out and keep in your purse to take shopping with you.

Apples or Pears? Price List to the Rescue!

Let's say you are trying to decide whether or not to buy apples in season at Kroger. Your plan is to eat some fresh and use the rest to make dried apples and applesauce for the pantry. However, pears are also in season during that time, and your neighbor will let you harvest his pears for free. Should you buy fewer apples? How many pears should you pick when there is limited pantry space and time for canning?

Take the lowest price you have found for each fruit in the last six months to determine your "top dollar" price. Different fruits will have different "top dollar" prices.

Apples- $1.00 per pound
Bananas- $0.80 per pound
Oranges- $1.50 per pound
Pears- $0.00 per pound
Strawberries - $1.00 per pound

If you are in a quandary whether to make applesauce or

pear sauce this year, it is only logical financially to make MORE pear sauce and LESS applesauce. Instead of apples being your primary autumn fruit, make pears the fruit of choice.

You do not have to have a fruit for every season. I make my free fruit last all year long! We have fresh fruit for about six months out of the year, and the other six months we eat frozen or canned fruit; it doesn't hurt us at all. In the meantime, we are saving hundreds of dollars per year by not purchasing fruit and just eating what we can get for free.

Berries or Berries... What Does it Matter?

One mom I know- we'll call her Jane- used to buy blueberries to put in the freezer. It was a yearly tradition, and the kids loved to eat frozen blueberries. One year they moved, however, and the new house had several mulberry trees on it. Jane spent June and July out in the mulberry orchard collecting berries. She was beside herself with the happiness of finding free fruit.

Later that summer, a friend asked her if she wanted blueberries. Jane said yes- of course she wanted some blueberries. It was kind of a tradition, after all. She ordered 20 pounds.

When the 20 pounds arrived at her house, she found out that they cost $2.00 per pound. It was hard to hand over the

$40.00 when she had just filled her freezer with FREE mulberries. After gathering free fruit, paying $2.00 per pound was almost painful. The kids didn't care whether or not they ate mulberries or blueberries. Both kinds were nutritious, and certainly in pancakes or smoothies the end result was almost the same.

The next summer, Jane had perfected her mulberry harvesting process. She made jam AND froze a lot of the berries. In July, blueberry season rolled around and prices had hiked to $2.50 per pound. "No way am I buying blueberries this year!" Jane said, saving herself an automatic $50.00.

Comparing Apples to Oranges

The price list differs from the price <u>book</u> in this: instead of comparing different prices of apples, for example, we will be comparing the lowest prices of ALL fruits. Note: the "top dollar" is the highest price I am willing to pay for any kind of fruit.

Overall Price List

Fruit- $1.00 per pound "top dollar":
      Apples- $1.00 per pound
      Bananas- $0.80 per pound
      Oranges- $1.50 per pound
      Pears- $0.00 per pound
      Strawberries - $1.00 per pound

After reviewing my price book, I have given every food category a "top dollar" that I am willing to pay.

Vegetables- $0.50 per pound "top dollar"
Beans- $0.60 per pound "top dollar"
Grains- $0.50 per pound "top dollar"
Meat- $1.00 per pound "top dollar"
Etc.

In order to consistently get the lowest price possible, we can't be picky about kinds. To save the MOST money, <u>only eat what you can buy for under a certain price.</u>

Using a price list for a guideline may sound boring or unfair ("I'll never eat pineapple again!"), but it is a habit you'll want to establish. In the past, you were probably buying fruit that was priced (per pound) all over the place, from free to $5.00 or more per pound, at an average of $2.50 per pound. If you buy 100 pounds of fruit per year and lower that average price to $0.75 per pound, you will have saved $175.00. And that is only on fruit.

That's not to say that you can NEVER buy something- like pineapple- that is more expensive than what the price list dictates. Just be careful to buy pineapples only when they are on sale and only for special occasions. Every pound of expensive fruit you buy brings the average price per pound of fruit up.

When you have finished your list, put it in your purse. When you go to the grocery store, refer to the list when you are wondering if something is a deal or not. You can also make a similar list with homemade food ingredients, and include the "homemade" price on your price list if that is the lowest.

The Power of Using a Price List

Thanks to my price list, I don't pay more than $0.50 per pound for rice, <u>regardless of what kind it is</u>. If you don't lump all rices together, you will start to think "this is a good price *for brown rice*" or "this is a good price *for wild rice*", and you will buy that rice even though it is much more expensive- on sale- than plain old white rice. Before you know it, you've unintentionally increased your standard of living, and white rice is no longer good enough because wild rice is "on sale" that week. I know that I can always get white rice in 20 lb. bags at Walmart for $0.45/lb. whenever I want. Therefore, it wouldn't make sense for me to buy a 1 lb. bag of rice (whatever kind it is) that is "on sale" for $0.69. The yearly savings are significant if I consistently buy rice that is $0.45/lb. or cheaper.

$0.89/lb. rice (1 lb. per week x 52 weeks): $46.28
$0.45/lb. rice (1 lb. per week x 52 weeks): $23.40

Savings on rice per year: **$22.88**

Imagine the power of a price list if you applied these rules to EVERYTHING on your shopping list. $20.00 doesn't seem like much, but remember that is only for a single item, for one person's consumption. Imagine the effect if applied to 50 different items for five, six or ten people.

Rice vs. Potatoes

So we've established that I can buy one pound of rice for $0.45. But what if I decide to use potatoes as my starch instead? I know I can buy a 10 lb. bag of potatoes for $3.94 at Walmart. This means that potatoes are $0.39 per pound... about a nickel cheaper than rice.

$0.45/lb. rice (1 lb. per week x 52 weeks): $23.40
$0.39/lb. potatoes (1 lb. per week x 52 weeks): $20.28

Savings by choosing potatoes over rice: **$3.12**

Of course we all want variety in our diets, but now we know that it is cheaper to make meals with potatoes than it is to make meals with rice. Which means we might have *two* potato-based meals per week, and only *one* rice-based meal.

You can do the same thing with vegetables, nuts, beans, beverages, desserts, and any other category that you can think of.

You don't have to stick hard-and-fast to your price list. I often buy expensive items and ingredients for the holidays, birthdays or vacation. But for the other 48 weeks of the year, I only buy things that cost less than my top dollar price.

Tip: Remember to consider waste in the "cost per pound". For example, rice is a little more expensive than potatoes, but every grain of rice can be eaten. If you are peeling a potato and throwing the peels away, how much of that 10 lb. bag is going to waste? The same idea holds true for bananas, stone fruit, bone-in meat and many other items.

I usually don't go so far as to calculate how much I'm paying for waste when buying meat or produce. However, if two hams are the same price and one of them is boneless, it might be smarter to pick the boneless ham.

Another thing you can do to counteract the cost of waste is to reuse or recycle it. Ham bones, for example, can be cooked with soup to add flavor to the dish (remove the bone before eating). Potato skins can be baked and used as an appetizer if they have been well scrubbed. Vegetable scraps can be frozen and then thawed to make vegetable stock (throw the scraps in a pot of water and boil for 30 minutes; add salt to taste). Orange peels can be boiled in water and used as potpourri, or soaked in vinegar to use in homemade cleaners. Wilted and sad-looking herbs can be made into pesto. Some vegetables, like carrots, celery or avocados, can even be re-grown from scraps. As a last resort, produce waste can always be composted or fed to chickens.

A Price List for Homemade Foods, Too

After you know the "top dollar" price you are willing to *buy* an item for, it's time to see if you should be making that item from scratch. Some foods commonly made at home are bread, granola, or cookies. You probably have recipes in your kitchen right now that you use on a regular basis. Some of these recipes are saving you money, but some of them are not.

To figure out the cost of your recipes, simply add up all of the ingredients on my price list/recipe calculator spreadsheet. You can get this spreadsheet for free on the "Printables & Downloads" page at www.therenaissancehousewife.com.

Comparing Cookies to Cookies

Several years ago, I figured out the price of every cookie recipe I had. After running each recipe through the calculator, I wrote the cost down on the recipe card. When I put all of the recipe cards next to each other and compared the prices, I was shocked. One of my least favorite cookies- oatmeal raisin- was actually quite expensive to make. One of my favorite kinds- peanut butter- was one of the cheapest. The ever-popular chocolate chip cookie cost twice as much to make as the less-popular but also yummy molasses cookies.

I have made a price list for homemade cookies, just like I have for all of the other food items that we buy.

My "price list" for homemade cookies looks like this:

$1.00-$2.00
Lemon Bars- $1.56

$2.00-$3.00:
Peanut Butter- $2.22
No-Bake Cookies- $2.61
Gingersnaps- $2.76
Walnut Frosties- $2.78
Sugar Cookies- $2.78
Molasses Crinkles- $2.78

$3.00-$4.00:
Mocha Chip- $3.07
Oatmeal Raisin- $3.84

$4.00-$5.50:
Chocolate Chip- $4.45
Monster Cookies- $5.17

If I'm in the habit of making cookies every week, my choice of cookie can have a profound effect on my yearly cookie spending.

Lemon bars once a week ($1.56 x 52): **$81.12**
Monster cookies once a week ($5.17 x 52): **$268.84**

Yearly savings by choosing lemon bars over monster cookies: **$187.72**. That is a lot of money saved by one simple change in the weekly menu.

When Should You <u>Buy</u> Cookies?

The price list also makes the question of "DIY or buy" easy to answer. If you see a box of cookies (or a cookie mix) for less than $1.00, it might be smart to buy it. There is no reason to feel guilty about buying cookies when it saves you time AND money.

Tip: When figuring the cost of a store-bought cookie mix, don't forget to add the price of the oil and egg that is often needed. Also, if you are going to buy a mix, choose one that already has chocolate chips or nuts inside of it. These can be the most expensive ingredients of cookie-making.

Sometimes it's hard to tell how many cookies will come out of a box mix. It is usually less than your standard homemade batch of cookies. If you have been asked to bake two dozen cookies for your child's class, then one box won't cut it, and you're better off to make an inexpensive variety of cookie from scratch. If you are just making cookies for your family or a potluck, though, the quantity is not as big of a deal. If your family is like mine, they will eat however many cookies you make, whether it is four or 24.

Capturing Bulk Savings

Monthly shopping, as opposed to weekly shopping, allows you to take advantage of bulk savings. If you have $10.00 to spend, then you will need to buy small packages in order to get everything you need for the week. But if you have $40.00 to spend, you will be able to buy bigger packages of those same items, and likely save some money along the way.

Start buying everything in the biggest package possible, <u>if</u> it's a better deal. Bigger containers don't always mean a better price. Sometimes, like in the case of barbecue sauce, the smaller bottles are cheaper. Many grocery stores have a "price per pound/oz./unit" listed on the shelf below the product. This will help immensely, as different packaging sizes and prices can be confusing.

Comparison of bulk packaged vs. non-bulk packaged food items per pound:

Flour: $0.34/lb. (5 lb. bag) vs. $0.34/lb. (25 lb. bag) = **0% savings**

Sugar: $0.50 lb. (4 lb. bag) vs $0.48/lb. (25 lb. bag) = **4% savings**

Rice: $0.50 lb. (2 lb. bag) vs $0.47/lb. (20 lb. bag) = **6% savings**

Beans: $1.05/lb. (2 lb. bag) $0.79/lb. (25 lb. bag) = **25% savings**

Cheese: $3.00/lb. (2 lb. package) vs $2.22/lb. (5 lb. package) vs. $2.00/lb. (10 lb. package) = **33% savings**

Chicken Quarters: $1.96/lb. (2-3 lb. package) vs $0.75 (10 lb. package) = **36% savings**

Ground Beef: $2.97/lb. (1 lb. package) vs $1.88/lb. (20 lb. package) = **37% savings**

You can see that buying one huge package vs. many small packages is not *always* a bargain. But in most cases you can save a little, and in some cases you can save a lot.

In order to find large quantities of food, think about who buys a lot of food, and shop where they shop. Amish people have large families, so they frequently own and patronize bulk food stores or produce auctions. Sometimes it is harder to find information about Amish stores and auctions because they send out postcards or other non-electronic forms of media. You may be able to find a map or phone number to the store online, and then you can stop in or make a phone call for more information. LDS (Church of Latter Day Saints, aka Mormon) families are encouraged by the denomination to keep both a 3-month supply and long term (items that last 30 years or more) food storage on hand, so they are frequent bulk buyers as well. Seventh Day Adventists put a lot of emphasis on physical health, so they often purchase health food in large quantities. One Seventh Day Adventist store that I like going to is Country Life Natural Foods. If you don't know anyone with these religious beliefs, start by running a Google search on "Amish Bulk Food [my state]" or "LDS food storage [my state]", etc. You don't have to be part of these churches to shop where they shop. And remember, always check your price list before assuming that buying at a bulk food store is a good deal.

Restaurant owners are also in the market for large quantities of food, so find out where they are buying all of their stuff. Start by running a Google search for "wholesale bulk food restaurant distributer market". Somebody has to supply schools, prisons, caterers, nursing homes and other institutions with a lot of cheap food. One place we enjoy shopping at is Gordon Food Service. However, even Walmart Supercenters have many items (rice, beans, flour, sugar, etc.) available at a discount in bulk.

Buying in bulk packages requires more money at the outset, but it is a great way to start saving 10-35% or more right away.

Buying Regular-sized Packages in Bulk

"Well that's nice," you say, "But how am I supposed to buy things like peanut butter or bread in bulk?"

You don't need to buy a one-gallon jar of peanut butter or order a pallet of bread to get a bulk discount. In fact, small containers are often a better deal than large ones when the smaller size is on sale. The concept of a pantry goes beyond "buy the biggest container possible".

Julie & Ginger Go Shopping

Julie and Ginger both buy ground beef, bread, eggs and peanut butter. Each week the grocery store offers $1.00 off on one of these items.

Monday morning, Julie walks into the store and picks up her ground beef, bread, eggs, and peanut butter. Peanut butter is on sale this week, so she saves $1.00. Woohoo!

Ten minutes later, Ginger walks into the store. Sale advertisement in hand, she walks past the ground beef, eggs and bread. Stopping at the peanut butter, she grabs one jar for each week of the month, and heads back to the checkout counter. Ginger saves $4.00.

You can see that Julie and Ginger are both eating and buying the same things, and both of them are paying attention to sales. Next week Julie will buy all four items again and be happy to save another dollar on her loaf of bread. Ginger, however, will buy four loaves of bread and nothing else, because she has ground beef in the freezer, plus eggs and peanut butter in the pantry from when *those* things were on sale.

At the end of the year, Julie will have saved $52.00 on her four grocery items. Ginger, however, will have saved $208.00.

That's the power of stocking a pantry.

Stocking Your Pantry at 50% Off

We don't want to buy one jar of peanut butter every week and only save $0.75 the one week that it was on sale. Instead, we buy ten jars of peanut butter during the one week it is on sale, and the other weeks we don't buy <u>any</u> peanut butter. Can you see how this essentially lowers our grocery bill by $0.75 *every week*?

If you find a great sale at a normal grocery store, stock up. Buy enough for a year if possible (<u>if</u> it will keep that long, or if you have the room for it in your pantry), or at least a couple months. In the United States, sales run in 12-week cycles, so if you buy enough for three months it will probably last until the next sale. Keep in mind, though, that prices rarely go down and are certain to go up. If something non-perishable is on sale, you might as well buy enough for a year. In the next six months, even the sale price could go up. A penny today is worth two pennies tomorrow.

Most of us are used to doing weekly shopping, buying the same (often non-perishable) items every week. There is nothing wrong with shopping every week, but instead of buying two items on sale and 18 that are not on sale, we need to ONLY be buying items on sale (or otherwise discounted), even if that means we are spending $40.00 on only two food groups during a given week.

As you can see, buying in bulk applies to more than just bulk packaging. Bulk buying means that when the price goes down, you buy a LOT. Then you don't buy <u>any</u> of that item until your stockpile starts to get low and you can find another bargain.

Changing from a "weekly grocery list" mindset to a "pantry shopping" mindset can at least cut your grocery bill in half.

Warning to Bulk Buyers:

It's tempting to use more of something when you buy in bulk (large packages OR shopping sales). "There is plenty here," you tell yourself, "so that means I can take a generous helping!" The savings from buying in bulk will be canceled out if you use more of the food item than you would have otherwise. For example, it is tempting to eat large chunks of cheese when you buy an entire wheel, as opposed to when you buy it in one or two pound blocks. In eating a small portion of the wheel, you won't realize that you just ate half a block- or a WHOLE block- of cheese in one sitting.

If you have kids, be aware that they too are susceptible to bulk eating. One of my readers sent me a picture of a crate full of apples, with several half-eaten ones lying on the table. "If I have six apples and hand them out to the kids, they will each eat their apple to the core," she explained. "But if I set out a half-bushel, I find half eaten apples all over the place."

One way to combat bulk eating is to immediately repackage the bulk item into normal-size bags or containers. The reader above also mentioned that just putting the large packages out sight can help as well.

Mistakes People Make With Bulk Buying

Some people buy in bulk *in addition to* their normal grocery budget. I see a lot of people go and buy insane amounts of everything from coconut oil to nuts and unrefined sugars and count it as a "one time purchase" or "special purchase" or "investment" outside of the normal grocery budget. Buying in bulk is not an excuse to make purchases that you otherwise couldn't afford. Instead, we must include bulk buying <u>inside</u> the budget.

The other mistake housewives make is to purchase a bulk amount of food, and forget a week later that they have *already spent* their rice/beans/flour money, and go back to buying beans every week. If you spend $50.00 on cheese in January and your weekly budget for cheese is $2.50, you cannot buy cheese for the next five months. If you forget about the huge wheel of cheese you bought in January and start buying smaller cheese packages again in March, you are actually spending <u>more</u> than originally planned.

The Bulk Buying Envelope

Have you ever heard of "the debt snowball"? It is a method of paying off debt in which you pay the smallest debt off first while making minimum payments on all of the others. After you have the first debt paid off, you put all of that money toward paying off the next smallest debt, while making minimum payments on the others. As you get the little debts paid off, more and more money is freed up to pay off the larger debts. Just like a snowball rolling down a hill, you gain momentum and pay off debt faster and faster as time goes on.

The six month bulk buying plan below works in the same way. First you will start with some "seed money" to buy a large bag of beans. The next month you won't have to buy any beans, so where will that money go? To fund the bulk purchase of rice! The next month you won't have to buy beans OR rice, so that money will be used to buy a large bag of flour. The idea is to buy one thing in bulk every month, using the savings from previous months of bulk buying. This will allow you to make large bulk purchases slowly, so you don't spend your whole budget on a 100 lb. sack of flour. The figures below are from my "Beginner's Grocery Budget" of $20.00 per person, per week. The bulk buying program includes common, useful food items you can buy in bulk from Walmart. The progression from month to month shows how bulk savings can add up. For simplicity's sake, my example plan is based on amounts for one person. A family of four could replace the word "month" with "week" to speed up the program.

Month 1: 20 lbs. Beans ($19.00)

Use the money you budgeted for beans ($4.00 per month) plus an extra $15.00 "seed money" (you can take this from another area in the budget; clothing, for example) to buy a 20 lb. bag of beans. The beans should last you at least six months.

Month 2: 20 lbs. Rice ($10.00)

Use the money you would have spent on beans ($4.00) plus the money you have budgeted for rice ($4.00) with $2.00 "seed money" from elsewhere in the budget, to buy a 20 lb. bag of rice. The rice should last you at least six months.

Month 3: 25 lbs. Flour ($8.00)

Use the money you would have spent on rice and beans ($8.00) to buy a 25 lb. bag of white flour. With the $4.00 you budgeted for bread and $1.00 from elsewhere in the budget, buy a small jar of bread yeast. These ingredients can be used to make bread for the next six months.

Month 4: 20 lbs. Chicken Quarters (two 10 lb. bags at $8.00 each)

Use the money you would have spent on beans, rice, and bread ($12.00) plus $4.00 out of the monthly meat allowance to purchase two 10 lb. bags of chicken quarters. This should last you two months.

Month 5: Eggs

Use the money you would have spent on beans, rice, bread, ($12.00) and 50% of the meat allowance ($8.00) to buy a box of five dozen eggs. **Note:** Eggs can be stored in a cool place for several weeks. They don't need to be kept in the refrigerator. The eggs should last over a month.

Month 6: Produce

Put the money you would have spent on beans, rice, bread, 50% of the meat budget and one dozen eggs ($21.50) in the "Bulk Buying Fund" envelope. When you find produce at $0.55/lb. or less, use the money to buy 40 pounds of produce. One large bell pepper weighs about ½ pound, so if you see peppers at $0.25 each, that is a good buy. Last year I found $0.25 peppers at a farmers market. You will probably only find prices this low when peppers (or any kind of produce) are in season, bought in very large quantities, damaged or starting to go bad. Theoretically you would buy the 40 pounds all at once, but in reality you will probably find it in smaller increments. This produce can then be preserved by freezing, canning, or cold storage. Used at the rate of two pounds per week, it should last one person five months. This should cut the monthly grocery budget by $8.00 per month.

Bulk Buying, Months 7-12

After six months, you will probably still have rice, beans, and possibly flour left over. You can start the snowball all over again, but this time you will start with $8.00 extra each month (until month 11) from the produce savings, plus $4.00 each from bread, beans and rice until they run out. The "extra" money at the end of each month can be put in the bulk buying envelope, in addition to money designated for items you already have at home (beans/rice/bread/etc.).

Month 7: $8.00 (produce savings) + $4.00 (beans savings) + $4.00 (bread savings) = $16.00 bulk snowball money - $10.00 (rice purchase) = $6.00 left over.

Month 8: $8.00 (produce savings) + $4.00 (rice savings) + $4.00 (bread savings) + $6.00 (leftover Month 1 money) = $22.00 bulk snowball money - $19.00 (beans purchase) = $3.00 left over.

Month 9: $8.00 (produce savings) + $4.00 (rice savings) + $4.00 (bean savings) + $3.00 (leftover Month 2 money) = $19.00 bulk snowball money - $13.00 (flour + yeast purchase) = $6.00 left over.

Month 10: $8.00 (produce savings) + $4.00 (rice savings) + $4.00 (bean savings) + $4.00 (bread savings) + $6.00 (leftover Month 3 money) + $8.00 (50% meat allowance) = $34.00 - $32.00 (3 bags chicken quarters) = $2.00 left over.

Month 11: $8.00 (produce savings) + $4.00 (rice savings) + $4.00 (bean savings) + $4.00 (bread savings) + $8.00 (meat savings) + $2.00 (leftover Month 4 money) = $30.00 bulk snowball - $16.00 (10 dozen eggs) = $14.00 left over.

Month 12:$4.00 (rice savings) + $4.00 (bean savings) + $4.00 (bread savings) + $8.00 (meat savings) + $6.00 (egg savings) + $14.00 (leftover Month 5 money) = $40.00 bulk snowball fund.

At the end of one year, you are starting out the month with beans, flour, bread ingredients, eggs, chicken, and $40.00 to spend on produce if you find a great deal. These are all things that you do not have to include in the budget. In this way, my beginner's budget of $20.00 per week can be cut down to $12.00 for at least a few months out of the year. Of course, you still need to keep making bulk purchases, so the beginner's budget cannot be cut permanently to $12.00. But remember, at this point we are only buying five grocery items in bulk. When everything is being purchased in bulk, chances are that the grocery budget can be lowered permanently. And that is without coupons, free food, or other strategies we will talk about in the coming chapters. Bulk purchasing, or stocking a pantry, is the foundation for a small food budget.

I won't write out a plan for the next five years of bulk purchasing, but you get the idea. At Month Six I have $20.00 to buy bulk produce. At Month 12 I have $40.00, which will buy TWICE as much produce as Month Six, therefore saving me twice as much money, so at Month 18 I will be able to buy $80.00 worth of produce in bulk. The more money you SAVE on different items, the more money you have to purchase things that will save you even more money.

Tip: In my one-year example above, I used bulk-packaged items from Walmart at their regular price. I chose these food items to get you in the habit of buying in bulk, but eggs, for example, are often cheaper to purchase by the dozen, on sale, than in bulk. When you have enough money saved for bulk buying, you can be flexible and buy eggs whenever they are on sale- not just during Month Five. Flexibility is the key to more savings.

Note for Advanced Readers: Those of you who already have a pantry established can refer to my "Sample Pantry List" and write down all of the things you are not buying in bulk yet. Instead of going through the 12 month bulk buying program above, you can just put 10% of your current food budget in the bulk buying envelope to either buy bulk packages (spices, etc.) or stock up on sale items (produce or meat) that are priced below your "top dollar" buying price. As you start purchasing even more of your grocery list in large quantities, plan on reducing your budget by at least 10% within a year's time.

How to Store Pantry Items

So you've started shopping for the pantry instead of weekly meals. You've just scored a HUGE deal and brought home an entire case of bananas/chicken thighs/butter/whatever and have NO idea how to make it last until the next sale. Here are some tips and tricks.

Meat: The easiest way to preserve meat is to just freeze it. Sausage, pepperoni, ham or other meats that will be used in small amounts can be cooked and then frozen. To freeze small amounts: use a gallon-size twist tie bag. Put a 1 cup portion (this is what I do for two people- adjust for your own family size) in the bag. Use a twist tie to close the bag as tight as possible. There will be a small lump of meat and a large amount of extra bag. After you've closed the bag, put another portion in the top of the bag. Close it off again. Keep doing this until you've used up the whole bag. When finished, the bag should look like a string of lumpy sausage links. <u>Note</u>: I always cook meat before freezing it in small portions. There is no reason to dirty a pan in order to cook such a small amount of meat.

Instead of buying "bacon" bits from the store, I cut real bacon into small pieces before I cook it. After cooking, the grease is drained off to use for frying eggs and such. The bits are frozen and used little by little. In this way, one pound of discount bacon can last for weeks.

If you run out of freezer space, you can also pressure can meat. In particular I like canning bone-in chicken legs (the ones you can find for $0.65/lb.) as well as chunk meat or stew meat. Pressure canning will make the tough, stringy stew meat nice and soft. It will also draw out minerals from the chicken bones and produce a wonderful gelatinous broth to use in soups.

When I bring home (or butcher) a lot of meat, I will spend an hour or two cutting it up, and then put into the freezer. If I am going to pressure can the meat, I put it back into the fridge after cutting. I might also sterilize jars at this time so they will be ready to use. The next day I will get out my pressure canner, jars, lids and rings, and spend the afternoon canning. Each jar fits between one and two pounds of meat (less for bone-in, more for ground or chunk meat) and my canner will hold seven quart jars. Pressure canning isn't a difficult thing to do and there is not a lot of hands-on time involved, but cooking time is usually an hour and a half, not including the time it takes the pressure canner to heat up (30 minutes or so). Then you have to let the canner cool down before you take the jars out (another hour or two). This is why I do the cutting one day and canning the next.

Tip: Many of my tightwad friends and relatives have had success re-using canning lids. This can save a lot of money if you are a frequent canner, especially in regards to wide-mouth lids, which tend to be more expensive. Conventional wisdom is NOT to re-use lids, so do this at your own risk. You can tell if the jar has sealed by pushing on the top of the lid. If it pops up and down, the jar has NOT sealed. Put any unsealed jars in the fridge and use

within the next week. Always smell
it, and always make sure to press
Occasionally a jar will un-seal e
which is why it is important to
Usually if a jar has unsealed
canned something that sho
canner (pumpkin, for example), 2,
canning method (open kettle canning o
an untested recipe.

Dairy: Again, freezing is the way to go. Milk can be
but I think it is a waste of freezer space and the texture is better
fresh.

Mozzarella cheese freezes very well. After buying a huge
brick, I will take it home and cut it into "chunks" for slicing and
eventually using on sandwiches. You can also shred mozzarella
before freezing, but it is optional.

Shredding with other cheeses, however, is NOT optional.
Other hard cheeses like cheddar will become crumbly after they
have thawed out, which makes slicing impossible. Therefore, I
always shred the cheese before freezing, or simply buy the
cheese already shredded.

Butter freezes excellently as well. Like cream cheese, it
can also last for several months in the fridge.

Sour cream, yogurt, cottage cheese and other dairy

ately do not freeze well or last several months.
make my own yogurt on a weekly basis with
rchase other dairy products I try to find them on
e cheapest brand without fillers.

Eggs: can be stored several weeks in a cool, dark place
a basement. You can tell an egg is too old to use if it floats
ter. Eggs can also be frozen, as long as you separate the
lks from the whites. If using for baked goods or scrambled
eggs, the yolks and whites can be mixed together with a knife
before freezing. Two tablespoons is equal to one egg.

Fruits: Fruits can be frozen, canned, dried or put into cold
storage. It all depends on the type of fruit and what you want to
do with it. Many fruits can be frozen and used for smoothies or
blender gelatin. They can also be sliced, dried and added to snack
mix, granola, etc. When it comes to canning, you can use apples
to make applesauce, berries to make jams and jellies, and most
fruits (with the exception of citrus or tropical fruit) can be made
into pie filling and used in fruit crisp.

Apples are one example of a fruit that can be put into cold
storage. Pick the best blemish-free apples you can find, and wrap
each one in newspaper. Put them in a box, making sure none of
them are touching each other, and then keep that box in a cold
(but not freezing) place, like a basement or unheated entry room.
I've had fresh apples last for months like this.

Tip: You don't have to own a "real" water bath canner in order to can small half-pint jars of jam or jelly. You can use a large pot (with lid) that has a wash cloth at the bottom. Use just as you would a regular water bath canner, but make sure the jars aren't directly touching the bottom of the pot (hence the washcloth), otherwise they will break. Your pot needs to be several inches taller than the jars; they need to be covered by at least one inch of water in order to seal properly. Sometimes I use this method when I only have a few jars to can. Perhaps the recipe didn't make very much, or perhaps some of the jars from my bigger batch did not seal correctly. Using a pot instead of the large water bath canner will save money on energy because you are boiling less water.

Some people water bath can using old salsa jars (with lids) or other non-standard glass jars with metal lids. I have not tried this because I have normal home canning equipment that is reliable and cost effective. It makes more sense to me than trying to keep track of 10 different kinds of jars, each with a different kind of lid. However, if you don't have access to regular home canning equipment, this could be an option to try.

A last option for fruit is to make it into wine or vinegar. This requires a little more skill and time, but will pay off for the adventurous homemaker or cook.

Vegetables: I prefer to freeze most vegetables, because with the exception of tomatoes or pickled items, most vegetables are low-acid. Therefore, they need the high heat of a pressure canner to make them safe to consume. The problem with pressure canned vegetables is that they lose a lot of vitamins and flavor in the canning process. Things like bell peppers, green beans or sweet corn are much better frozen. I freeze sweet corn and green beans in quart-size freezer bags, but the bell peppers are sliced and frozen in a gallon size bag. Whenever I need some for stir fry, I just grab a handful out of the bag and put the rest back into the freezer. It cuts back on bag use and prevents waste.

The good news is that many vegetables can be kept in cold storage. Onions, garlic, sweet potatoes, white potatoes, carrots, winter squash and many others can just sit on the shelf for weeks or months until you are ready to use them. As I write this it is July, and I still have a perfectly good winter squash from last year sitting in the back room.

I remember one time a friend of ours got a whole pallet full of potatoes for free and set them in our back yard for any takers. We had friends and family come and take their fill, but there were still a LOT of good potatoes left out there. Most of them had one or two bruise marks on them, and I knew they wouldn't last in cold storage. I decided instead to peel and cube the potatoes, and then pressure can them to use in soups or hash. While it was more work than just letting the potatoes sit in the pantry, I was able to salvage about 20 lbs. of free potatoes. Because they were pressure canned, the pieces came right out of the jar already cooked. It was so convenient that they were already cut up and ready to use at a moment's notice.

Grains & Beans: Almost all grains will do fine stored in five gallon buckets with lids. They will last for years that way. However, for convenience's sake I like to pressure can 3-6 months' worth of dry beans so that they are cooked and ready to use when I need them.

Smaller amounts of grains and beans can be stored in one-gallon pickle jars or regular mason jars. We got our one-gallon jars for free from a local pizzeria. All you have to do is ask.

Breads: Breads bought on sale can be frozen. I will also mention that many store-bought breads are full of preservatives and will last longer than the "best by" date before starting to mold or get stale.

Baking supplies: Most of these are non-perishable and can be stored in the pantry at room temperature. Just make sure to keep them in air-tight containers so that bugs and moisture cannot ruin them.

Random baking or pantry items can be organized in small containers bought from the dollar store. They often have a wide selection of baskets, boxes, tubs or other small containers that are pretty but also functional and easy to clean.

Herbs & Spices: I prefer to dry most of my herbs and spices (or buy them that way). Like baking supplies or beans, dried seasonings can last for years, though admittedly the quality will go down every year, especially if they are exposed to light.

Fresh ginger root will mold if left in the refrigerator. Instead, freeze the whole root. To use, grate the frozen root until you have the desired amount. Put whatever is left back into the freezer.

Eating Healthy on a Budget

Before we move any further along in our savings journey, I want to answer a question that is bound to come up.

Can you have a healthy diet on $10.00 per week?

The short answer is yes, you can eat <u>relatively</u> healthy on $40.00 per person, per month. You can eat very healthy on that amount if you employ some of the advanced strategies I mention, like organic gardening, bartering, or keeping a milk goat. If you think eating healthy means buying a bunch of prepackaged health food from a store, then NO, you cannot afford that.

Heath and frugality are often competing priorities. One of the fastest ways to go over budget is to be so focused on buying "health" food that you forget about saving money. I come across a lot of frugal mom bloggers who try to be frugal by shopping sales, foraging, etc, but whatever they save on produce or meat they automatically spend on fancy sugar substitutes and gluten-free flours. Even when people make their own gluten free flours, the price for buying almonds to make it with totally cancels out the other efforts to save. One Youtube housewife I enjoyed watching spent only $100.00 per month on groceries for five people. Another one boasted about spending "just" $600.00 per month on "groceries and health" for four people... and this lady was a homesteader! The difference between the two moms is that one of them was extremely focused on buying health food and supplements. The other was not, even though both ladies were trying to have a gluten free, relatively healthy diet.

Organic or Not Organic?

Whether or not to buy organic is another question that we have to deal with these days. If your goal is to save money, don't buy organic. There are many ways to get organic food for cheap or even free. Gardening is a great way to get organic food for pennies. I've also seen organic processed foods and gluten free products at discount stores, just because the box is dented or slightly over the best by date.

Do I think organic is better? Yes. Would I pay twice as much for it? No.

If you want to be healthy, start with the basics. Eat more vegetables. Drink water, cut out processed sugar and sweet baked goods. Far too often I see families eating organic cheetos and cold cereal because they think it is healthier than non-organic scrambled eggs or oatmeal. It is not.

In short, the key to eating healthy on a small budget is... DON'T BUY HEALTH FOOD. You can get it for free or on sale or by some other means, but on such an extreme budget you can't afford to buy stuff marketed as "healthy".

Fitting a Special Diet Plan to the Budget

With any special diet plan, there are methods and principles. My theory is to follow the principles, but fit the methods to your own situation. This takes some creative thinking at times. It also takes some cooking skills and knowledge. Before designing your own methods, you must realize that the makers of almost every diet book or plan out there- grain free, sugar free, gluten free, meat free, you name it- are trying to make money. Most of them have specialized products that you can only buy from their website, and guess what? You will stay fat and sick unless you buy those products that are an integral part of the plan! Be wary of marketing. There are alternative ways to be paleo/gluten-free/low-fat/high-fat without buying a load of expensive health foods. I'm inspired by the diet of Native Americans, who lived entirely on what I have growing in my own figurative back yard. Deer, rabbit, maple syrup, cattails, sumac, and so much more. Certainly they managed to live and thrive without coconut oil or almond flour. Acorn flour, anyone? Eh, there must not be any profit in acorns.

Personally, I try to cook with mostly homegrown or homemade un-processed foods. Ideally this diet has as little sugar and as many nutrients as possible. Believe it or not, a relatively Nourishing Traditions/THM/Paleo/Gluten-free/overall healthy diet can be followed with only $15.00 per person, per week, using the following guidelines. Advanced techniques will get this down to $10.00 per week, but you'll have to do a lot of work to get there. I'm not a purist, so my budget is lower. For example, instead of using honey for all of my desserts, I still use white sugar, but just make less dessert. I don't buy anything organic. Below are some tips and tricks I use to eat healthy for less.

#1: Stop Baking

I mean it. Just stop making meals that include bread. That way if you're gluten free, you don't have to buy specialty flours. This will cut out many carbs for most people (donuts, cake, cookies, pastries, sweet breads, white breads) on a low carb diet. It will also cut out jam, peanut butter, and other fattening/expensive condiments that tend to be served with bread. Sweet dessert-type baked goods also use a lot of butter, which is rather expensive. I buy tortillas and make pizza crust, but that is about the extent of my baking.

#2: Stop Making Dessert

How are we going to survive without dessert? Actually, we may have a BETTER chance of surviving without dessert. Show me a family whose table is (or was, at one point) full of desserts, and I will show you potbellies and mouths full of dental cavities. Desserts are fun for special occasions, but putting them in the weekly menu is probably not a good idea. Between church, potlucks, weekends away and now baking for the farmers market, my husband and I have plenty of dessert. I just don't make cookies a part of my regular meal plan. At $3.00-$5.00 per batch, per week, that's up to $260.00 per year spent on only ONE baked good. If you're trying to follow a special diet plan, I'll guarantee that dessert is where you'll spend all the money. Honey, not to mention cane sugar, maple syrup, stevia, xylitol and other "healthy" sweeteners are very expensive, especially when you are using several cups' worth in one sitting. If you must have dessert, make it fruit-based. Actually, fruit all by itself makes a wonderful dessert, if you stop using it as a snack (see #8).

#3: Stop Using So Much Butter

My husband and I use no more than a stick of butter per week. This is because I don't do any baking and use free animal fat (chicken, bacon grease) to fry things in.

#4: Stop Using Nuts

And this includes peanut butter. Some groups claim that unsoaked nuts cause cavities anyway. My husband likes almonds on his granola, but other than that I don't cook with nuts. Not baking (see #2) nearly eliminates my need for nuts. I know that trail mixes are popular snack foods, but apart from being unhealthy (many mixes include candy and pretzels), nuts and dried fruit are very expensive compared to more nutritious snacks like yogurt, carrot sticks, or even fruit smoothies.

#5: Utilize Wild Edibles

Instead of buying kale for smoothies, walk outside and

grab a handful of lambsquarter leaves or other wild green. Not only are these greens available April-October, but they are absolutely 100% free and are chock full of nutrients just like kale is. Greens, fruit, and herbs (for tea and medicinal use) and nuts can be found in abundance in the great outdoors. Some can even be frozen, pickled, canned, or dried for the pantry! If you live in town, ask a friend or relative if you can "shop" on their country property. But even small yards in town will provide you with dandelions, plantain, chickweed, lambsquarter, and other nutritious "weeds". If your lawn isn't big enough for a garden, there is always room for a weed patch somewhere.

The scope of this book is too small for a detailed guide on foraging. I have included uses and Latin names for the plants that I mention, but for sake of brevity I have left out pictures, cooking directions and detailed descriptions. You can learn more about the free wild foods I mention by poking around the "Foraging" page at www.therenaissancehousewife.com. I chose to list some wild edible plants in this book just to give you a taste of how much food is out there, hiding in hedgerows, backyards and roadsides. If you are serious about foraging, go to the library and find a book on wild edibles. These books will help you identify the plants safely and cook them in an appetizing way. Some of the books on my shelf include Bradford Angier's *Field Guide to Edible Wild Plants*, Pascal Baudar's *The New Wildcrafted Cuisine*, and an older volume from 1960 titled *Using Wayside Plants* by Nelson Coon.

Some of you may be wondering whether it is worth your

time to learn about foraging. Even if you can only save a few dollars per week by foraging for food, the knowledge you'll gain is applicable to many areas. Eventually you will learn how to use plants for MORE than just food. Many of the wild edibles can also be used for herbal medicine, dyeing cloth, flower arranging, cleaning and making everything from dolls to insect repellent and odor eliminator. Right now I am learning about how to use these same wild plants as free food for my goats and chickens. Foraging is not just a skill that will save money on food; it will save in many other areas.

#6: Utilize Organ Meats and Chicken Feet

I know this tip is NOT popular, but that's why you can get organs and feet for so cheap. Nutritionally, they are a big bang for the buck. Organs can be ground up and added to sausage or other flavored meats, and feet can be prepared and made into gelatinous broth quite easy, for $0.15 per quart, by simple pressure canning. You can read about this on my blog. Many people use the carcass for broth, but broth made in a crock pot cannot be canned (and still retain its gelatinous properties) like chicken-feet broth. Find organs and feet at a butcher shop or find a chicken-butchering friend. Organs can sometimes be found at the grocery store.

#7: Drink Only Free Beverages

Most of the time this is water. It can also include milk if you have a goat or cow, herbal tea if you forage or garden, and possibly kombucha or other fermented drinks on special occasions. Kombucha costs something like $0.25 per quart to make. Only drinking free beverages completely eliminates soda, alcohol, milk, fake milk, juice and other expensive drinks. Most drinks that you pay for are horrible for teeth and waistline. Store-bought milk has had many of the beneficial enzymes cooked out of it anyway. At $3.00 per gallon, a glass of milk costs $0.38. Drinking two glasses per day, that's $277.00 per year... for one person. Imagine how much it would cost for a whole family! If you are going to buy milk, it is better used for making yogurt.

#8: Only Eat Free Fruit

If you're getting free fruit, it means that you grew or foraged it yourself, or got it from a friend. This means the fruit was local, and possibly organically grown. Bonus points! Fruit is one of the more expensive parts of a diet. Most people consider fruit a "healthy" snack, but vegetables are better because they don't spike blood sugar or encourage cavities. Vegetables also contain plenty of vitamin C just like fruit. Honestly, one can survive without much fruit. I use fruit for smoothies and dessert, but that's about it. For our purposes, one strawberry patch can provide a year's worth of fruit, let alone all of the raspberries, mulberries, cherries, pears and apples that also grow on our property. I would rather sell the fruit (fresh or made into jam) and use that income to buy meat. If you can't find free fruit, only buy when prices drop below a certain price per pound- perhaps $0.50 per pound.

And don't be a sucker for the dried fruit in health stores. Dried fruit spikes blood sugar even more than fresh fruit, and most of it has added sugar for taste and sulphur as a preservative. If you really want dried fruit, dry some from your garden.

Less Spending = Better Health

If you're trying to save money and eat healthy, the hardest thing to let go of will be the belief that you can never be healthy unless you have X product every day; extra-virgin coconut oil, chia seeds on your organic oatmeal, pastured eggs, you name it. Diet books and TV shows have duped us into thinking that we have to *buy stuff* in order to be healthy. When I buy something from my favorite bulk food store, I literally <u>feel</u> healthy. I feel like I'm making a great investment in myself and my future progeny. Then the stuff gets hidden in the back of my cupboard and I never use it. But I still feel like I'm being healthy just for having it in my house. Isn't that crazy? Even if I never use the de-fatted peanut butter, xylitol, glucommanan powder, or almond flour, I've tricked myself into thinking it's an "investment", whereas a daily walk or bike ride can wait. *Maybe I'll exercise after I'm done reading one more article about essential oils.* Click, click, add to cart. $200.00 later.... time for a bike ride. *Oh bummer, now it's raining.* Time to read another article! *It's too late to make a healthy dinner, so I might as well just have cookies.*

We need to think about healthy eating in a logical way, not an emotional way. Most people eat certain health foods because some health guru told them they would look like [insert celebrity here] if only they followed "the plan". They are eating the health foods because of that illusion, NOT because it is the least expensive, most healthy way to eat.

Lastly, it's important that you have some kind of meal plan, lest you end up eating $2.00 protein bars every afternoon because you don't want to cook anything for dinner. It doesn't have to be fancy. Take the protein bars off your grocery list and buy a dozen eggs instead. Boil them up at the start of the week. By default, you will end up eating the eggs instead of the protein bars. It will be better for you (no sugar, preservatives, or soybeans), and cheaper. Re-evaluate your eating habits and see if there are any other small changes to make. You could save hundreds of dollars (and maybe some teeth) per year by replacing a PB & J meal with a rice and beans meal. I've laid out a very simple weekly meal plan in my book, *Pizza Night.*

Ultimately, you'll have to decide how much of a priority it is for you to buy health food, and ask if that is worth the money. Money can be used for a lot of things, including education, travel, buying a home, paying off debt, or giving to charities that feed orphans in Africa or stop human trafficking. If you asked me, I'd say that all of those things are more important than buying health food. Those of you without special health needs should consider not buying health food at all. Note that I said "buying health food" and not "eating healthy". Eating healthy on a shoestring budget is entirely possible, though it might take some ingenuity and work to get there.

Multi-level Marketing Supplements

While we are talking about health food, I'd like to address the topic of nutritional supplements. Supplements themselves are not necessarily expensive, but I want to point out an obvious budget-buster that many frugal people indulge in anyway: nutritional supplements sold through multi-level marketing (also called direct sales, "home-based businesses" or network marketing) companies.

Apart from the fact that MLM products are almost always overpriced, the main issue I have with these supplements is that they're bought on a "subscription" or "membership plan". Instead of paying $300.00 one time for a water filter, you are paying $3.00-$10.00 every single day for shakes or candy bars or pills or whatever form the supplement comes in. Even the cheaper MLM products will cost twice as much per day as your groceries, if you are trying to eat for $10.00 per week. Lowering your grocery bill is pointless if you turn around and spend $100.00 or more every month for something your body probably does not need (and sometimes will not even benefit from).

An Example of MLM Spending

Several months ago, many people I knew were into an MLM company that sold a crimson-colored drink powder that supposedly helped with weight loss, improved energy, cured sugar and caffeine "addiction", reduced inflammation, fixed gut issues and much more. The product cost $100.00 per person, per month (unless you bought several of the products, which would cost more). Being the extreme frugalite that I am, I decided to try and make my own "pink drink". I looked up the active ingredients, and bought them at Walmart in pill form. The coloring used was beet root, so instead of purchasing beet root powder, I just took some canned beets out of the pantry and put them in the blender with the crushed pills.

Apart from tasting absolutely terrible (thanks to the real beets), my homemade drink revealed something to me. In making my own supplement, I had to research all the ingredients, all the side effects, recommended daily allowances, and possible hazards associated with each. And I did not like everything I saw. I was scared to try my own concoction after mixing up a bunch of pills intended for diabetics (I am not a diabetic). Yet many of my perfectly healthy and not-even-overweight friends were spending hundreds of dollars to put the same ingredients into their bodies month after month.

Nobody on a $10.00 per week budget can afford any kind of MLM supplement unless they are going to recruit their friends into buying the overpriced product. I think there are better ways to save money than by getting your friends to spend theirs.

Buying the Store Brand

As I mentioned in the Beginner's Budget section, if you want to continue buying name brands on a regular basis, the $10.00 per week budget is not for you. One mistake I see many frugal people making is buying name brand products. Perhaps "Big J" peanut butter is $0.35 off this week, or they think it tastes better or is healthier than Walmart peanut butter. The dirty little secret is that most store brands are nearly identical to name brands. They can be grown on the same farm, shipped to the same factory and simply labeled differently.

Why the price difference, then? Store brands don't have to pay for marketing, so they can pass those savings on to their customers. Have you ever seen a TV ad for Walmart fruit snacks? Me neither. And oftentimes, Walmart peanut butter is cheaper than Big J *even if* the Big J is on sale or bought with a coupon.

I'll admit, sometimes the store brand does taste different. And sometimes the very cheapest of the cheap food has fillers or isn't even real food (cheese is sometimes soy "cheese product", for example). But if you are worried, check the label or do a taste test.

Klondike vs. Store Brand

After arguing about whether Klondike or store brand ice

cream sandwiches were better, Hubs and I decided to try both and have some friends over to see which ice cream bar was the best. Hubs was 100% sure that the Klondikes would be superior. My hypothesis was that the store brand would be equal in quality. But even before the wrappers were taken off, the two were obviously very different. The store brand sandwiches were smaller, and as the wrappers were taken off we could see that the off brand had much darker chocolate coating than the Klondike. When we cut open the ice cream bars, the Klondike had a thin, even chocolate coat, with rich, creamy ice cream. The store brand sandwich had an ugly, uneven, thick chocolate coat with lighter, airier ice cream on the inside.

I was shocked to see how different the two ice cream bars looked and tasted, but even though they were different, Hubs and I came to the same conclusion that both brands were good. I preferred the lighter ice cream in the off-brand, but liked the chocolate coating in the Klondike.

If both ice cream bars are good, it would only make sense to buy the off brand, which costs less money. Likewise, if there are two brands of tortillas that cost the same and one tastes better, we will buy the one that tastes better! But in general, we tend to buy off-brands and not name brand foods.

Utilizing Government Assistance

If you are in the position to receive free food through the SNAP/EBT program or other financial aid program (like WIC, for example), then there is really no reason why you shouldn't. Some people have an ethical issue with being on "welfare", but I don't understand why hard working, tax-paying people would let free food just sit on the table, so to speak. Some government programs are open to even average-income families (especially for those with several children).

Some things you should know before applying for assistance: many programs have requirements regarding assets (SNAP funds are unavailable for those with more than $2250.00 in the bank, for example), income and employment. But if you are having a hard time finding money for groceries, it is definitely worth looking into.

SNAP Benefits: The maximum allotment for a single person is $194.00. For a family of four, the maximum allotment is $649.00. On our $10.00 per week plan, a family of four would be spending $160.00. A family on the $10.00 per week plan could easily pay for groceries AND build up a sizeable pantry on food stamps alone. One thing I love about the SNAP program is that it allows for the purchase of seeds and plants for your vegetable garden. The money is free anyway, but when you use it to buy seeds and grow a garden, the dollar you would have spent on a pound of carrots can be used to grow 10 pounds of carrots.

Double Up Food Bucks is an offshoot of the SNAP/Bridge Card/EBT program. Participants are given special coinage to use their benefits at local farmers markets. For every EBT dollar you use at the market for fruits and vegetables, they will give you a bonus dollar to use on produce, up to $20.00 per week. That means that if you see a quart-sized box of apples priced at $3.00, you will only have to spend $1.50 of your monthly SNAP money to buy it... which means the apples are essentially 50% off. Keep in mind though, that many farmers markets are overpriced. Ask yourself, "Are the grocery store apples cheaper than $1.50 per quart?" If so, you are better off buying apples at the grocery store with your regular SNAP benefits.

The main problem with the DUFB program is that once your EBT benefits are exchanged, they must be spent at the farmers market. Oftentimes I see people during the last hour of the market frantically trying to spend the last of their "free" DUFB money, not realizing that $20.00 spent at the grocery store might go farther than $40.00 spent at the farmers market. I understand the point of the program- to encourage people to buy more produce- but for the savvy shopper, EBT funds can be better used elsewhere. That being said, for someone who doesn't have a garden, DUFB is a great way to find fruits and vegetables for preserving and putting into the pantry. Occasionally there ARE good deals at the farmers market, and if you can get 50% off on something that is already a deal, by all means do it!

WIC Benefits: Free food available through WIC includes milk, juice, breakfast cereal, cheese, eggs, fruits and vegetables, whole wheat bread, fish, dried or canned beans, and peanut butter. To apply for WIC, the household must include a pregnant or nursing mom, and/or children under the age of five. There are also income restrictions. For example, a household with one pregnant mother expecting one child must earn less than $29,471.00 per year (at the time of this writing) in order to qualify for WIC. The same example would apply for a family with two small children (without a pregnant mother). For young families who haven't established careers yet, I think applying for WIC would be a good way to save money on groceries and get ahead financially.

Free School Breakfast & Lunch: At the time of this writing, a family of four with a household annual income of less than $31,590.00 is eligible for free school lunches. Families earning between $31,591.00 and $44,955.00 per year are eligible for reduced price lunches. However, depending on which state you live in, a school lunch can cost between $1.25 and $3.00. Even a 50% reduction could leave you paying more for a school lunch than a homemade one, especially if you are following the principles in this book.

Food Pantry: Though not government programs, many communities and/or churches have some kind of food pantry program for those who need help getting out of a tough financial situation. Food pantries are more likely to give away non-perishable goods like pasta or canned food.

Where to Shop

Obviously there are many places where you can shop for food. Before we get started on individual stores, though, we need to remember that FREE food is the most frugal food. In order to cut groceries down to $10.00 per week and still have a nutritious, flavorful diet, we will need to utilize as much free food as possible.

Shop Local... Really Local

I believe that the best place to shop is in your backyard or garden, where the meat and produce is as fresh and healthy (and cheap!) as possible. I'm able to get strawberries, raspberries, apples, pears, cherries, sweet corn, green beans, lettuce, squash, tomatoes, peppers, broccoli, basil, sage, fennel, dill, mints, cilantro and garlic from my own property for mere pennies (if not for free). With these ingredients, I'm also able to make extremely cheap sauces, condiments, spices and herbal teas. We have a small hobby farm, so by selling off some of the goods I'm able to get eggs, milk and poultry for free or steeply discounted most of the year. These are all items that I don't normally have to buy at a grocery store.

I would highly encourage anyone reading this book to try gardening. You don't have to have a huge garden plot- even growing one or two things will save money. Other side benefits of gardening include outdoor activity, some free Vitamin D and free exercise, and the more time you spend gardening, the less time you will spend shopping or otherwise paying for entertainment. Gardening is fun in and of itself.

One concern in regards to gardening is the cost of water for those in urban areas. Because we live in the country, it is free for me to water the garden. But for those of you who do pay for water, www.hunterwater.com has a lot of tips for saving on water usage. Another site I love is www.theprudenthomemaker.com. The lady who runs the site lives in California where water is rather costly, and yet she keeps up a beautiful backyard garden that provides fruit, flowers, vegetables and herbs for her family most of the year. There are many gardening methods that use less water- for example, deep-watering (as opposed to the more common shallow watering) and using heavy mulch. However, there are also ways to recycle *used* water, so you are not paying to water your garden at all. Shower or bathtub water is great to use for watering plants, as long as you have not put a whole lot of bubble bath or stuff in it. You can also collect rainwater from your house roof to use for watering plants.

Bartering

There are other ways to get free food. For example, perhaps you have room for a garden, but not animals. By planting some extra produce, you can trade it for local meats or other more hard-to-get items. One lady I know was able to get high quality milk (valued at around $10.00 per gallon) by trading vegetables and poultry with the farmer. Though she may not have been able to afford it in money, this lady used a few dollars' worth of seeds to "buy" hundreds of dollars' worth of health food for her family. Most likely, there is a way you can do the same thing.

But the free food doesn't stop there. Perhaps you don't even have room for a garden. Do you have a friend who does? I know there are many gardening families (us included) who travel during the summer and miss harvesting certain items. We are happy to offer this produce to family and friends if they are willing to come and get it. Some people have too much and will just give it away.

Do the Work and Split the Bounty

Just recently, a cow-milking neighbor had more milk than he knew what to do with. He didn't want the seven gallons or more going to waste, so he looked for someone who would make cheese. I offered to do the job, and got to keep half of the cheese. You can use this same concept for canning or other types of food processing as well.

Do Hobby Farms Save Money?

Perhaps you have thought about getting backyard

chickens, or even animals for milk or meat. Many folks wonder if this is actually a frugal thing to do. It is a valid question- you might be getting "free" eggs, but you are still paying for feed, shelter, medical care and all of the other costs associated with keeping animals.

If you are thinking about starting a hobby farm, be careful to keep track of how much you spend. Also, make sure you are feeding the same amount every day, and try cutting back on feed to see if it helps or hurts. Many people are feeding their animals too much. You can also give alternative feeds (native plants or weeds), and I like mixing the feed half and half with corn to cut down on the price.

After several months, you will know roughly how much the animals cost per month to feed. When I first started with chickens, I figured out that my "free" eggs were costing at least $1.75 per dozen. After some manipulation with feed stuffs and amounts, laying production improved and my cost per dozen went down to about a dollar. However, the eggs were still not free.

A month or two later, I started collecting more eggs than we could eat, and needed to start selling some. I decided to charge $2.00 per dozen, which was a decent but not-too-expensive price for home grown eggs. Once the word got out, I had more customers than I had eggs for!

In two months' time, I was selling enough eggs to pay for

the cost of keeping my chickens. That meant that the eggs I didn't sell were truly free for my husband and I to use. This is how we get "free" eggs. I do have to sell three or four dozen eggs every week in order to get my one or two dozen per week free. If I don't sell that much (and I can't during the winter time), we are still paying for eggs.

How to Fund a Hobby Farm

Any farm animal you keep will require money, unless you have found out how to feed animals for free (in which case, please let me know!). Until then, keeping animals will only give you <u>discount</u> meat/milk/eggs/etc., and not *completely free* food. If you want completely free food from your own animals, it will be necessary to sell some of the bounty.

I have a neighbor who raises pigs. In order to get a free pig for her family, she raises one pig to eat and one pig to sell. I pay for my animals by selling things at a farmers market, and also by selling offspring. For example, my milk goat needs to have kids every spring in order to keep producing milk. I keep the kids until they are weaned, and then I can sell them. Bucks are worth $50.00 each, and does are worth about $150.00-$200.00. My two goats (one buck and one doe) cost about $8.00 per month to keep, or $96.00 per year. Selling the kids and some soap at the farmers market is more than enough to pay for their keep, which means we get to drink all of the milk for free.

Dumpster Diving

I don't live in the city, so I don't have any experience in this area. I do have friends who have successfully dumpster dived for food, though, so I thought I'd mention it. In my research for this book, I found a fascinating documentary called "Dive!" about dumpster diving for food and living off the waste of others. Obviously there are some safety precautions to be aware of when dumpster diving for food, but I will leave that to another book, as I have no experience to speak from. One interesting (and funny) book I read about dumpster diving is *The Art and Science of Dumpster Diving*, by John Hoffman.

Choosing Where to Shop

My husband and I like shopping at our local Walmart Supercenter, for reasons I will tell you later. Whatever store you choose to shop at, keep in mind the following:

1. It is better to choose one place and stick with it, than to stop at six different stores every week to look for deals. You will end up spending a lot more time, gas, and money on things that were never on your list to begin with. We have one store that we shop at all of the time (Walmart), and a few others that I go to once in a while to check prices on certain items. I just do not have the time to shop at, and monitor sales for, more than one store on a regular basis.

2. Go shopping alone, when you are full and wide awake. Morning is a good time to shop because it is often less crowded. I enjoy shopping with my husband (he finds some good deals), but we often end up buying things like ice cream, candy or donuts. I am sure it is also hard to say "no" to children or friends as well. On the other hand, sometimes my husband is in a hurry to leave, in which case I end up buying <u>less</u> than I would by myself.

3. Try to limit shopping trips to every other week, especially if there is a lot of driving involved. I have heard of a few exceptions, but most of the time people spend more money when they shop more often. I know it is true for myself. If we miss a week of shopping, I just cook with what we *do* have and everything turns out fine.

4. Find out the store's coupon policy. Some stores have "double coupon" days, where they will redeem twice the value of your coupon. Other stores, like Walmart, have a price matching policy and will match the price of any competitor offering the item at a lower price. Certain stores will also honor manufacturer's coupons, which are different than store coupons. Being able to use both types of coupons at your grocery store might allow you to save even more money.

5. If you're still establishing a pantry and working on a price list, watch sales. Ignore most processed foods, but keep an eye out for fruits, vegetables and meat. Some stores will have sales listed online, as well as any available coupons. Check online sales before you make your grocery list.

6. Use rebate apps on your phone (Ibotta or Checkout51, for example) for items that you buy regularly. I only use "any brand" rebates. That way I can buy the very cheapest brand and still use the rebate, which leaves me paying bottom-dollar. I often use rebates for bread, milk, pasta, and fruits or vegetables. Ibotta offers these rebates for a whole slew of stores, including the Dollar Tree. One neat trick is to use $0.25 rebates to buy quantities of produce that cost less than $0.25. For example, two carrots, one tomato, one chili pepper or a banana are some things you can buy for less than $0.25. When you use a rebate on these items, they are essentially free. I like to save up my bananas in the freezer for smoothies and use the tomato and other produce as accents to a meal.

7. Try to get all of the groceries unloaded at the checkout counter quickly so you can catch any mistakes that come up on the receipt right away. Buying a lot of sale items (common if you are shopping for your pantry) makes it more likely that a mistake will occur, on the part of the cashier or on your part because you THOUGHT something was on sale but it wasn't. Clear up any mistakes and overcharges immediately.

If you are shopping to be frugal, pick no-frills stores like Walmart, Aldi, or Save-a-Lot. If you don't have one of these stores (or one like it) near you, pick a good chain grocery store to patronize. Chain stores are more likely to have bulk items, store brands, and sales, which are essential to establishing a good pantry. Here are some places you should NOT do your regular weekly shopping at because they sell mostly more expensive items:

1) High-end grocery stores like Whole Foods or Trader Joe's.
2) Farmers markets. These often cater to high-income families by selling organic, local, etc.
3) Convenience stores or gas stations.

Why We Shop at Walmart

My husband and I are very loyal Walmart Supercenter shoppers. There are many reasons why we shop there, but mostly because the savings are HUGE. I have friends who don't shop at Walmart, supposedly for moral or political reasons. I think this is sad because many of them could really use the extra money. Boycotting Walmart may be the "in" thing to do, but is it the smartest thing? Will it help you achieve your personal goals? Will it help you send your kids to college or take longer vacations as a family? If you are anti-Walmart, I challenge you to carefully scrutinize your priorities and ask if it is really your conscience, or if it's just ego that is keeping you from the savings.

For some reason, society has demonized Walmart in particular, but it is okay to shop at other large chain stores like Kroger or Meijer. Are we really so naïve to think that the quality of bread at Kroger is better than the bread at Walmart? Especially when both stores carry many of the same brands? Do we really think that Kroger employees have a better life stocking shelves than Walmart employees stocking shelves? It all depends on the local people that are working there as staff. I know I have been treated much worse by staff at our local Kroger than at Walmart. It's not about the store- it's about the staff. As for the "poor" hourly wage and benefits for Walmart workers, I would venture to say that Walmart benefits are comparable to those of other large chain stores.

Don't think you are a better person by shopping at a "local" large chain grocery store instead of Walmart. That is like thinking Burger King is healthier than McDonalds.

Now that we have all excuses removed, I can talk about why I grocery shop at Walmart almost 100% of the time. Keep in mind that a majority of our food is produced at home, so we're only buying a few items at Walmart.

1. You can use gift cards there. My husband spends thousands of dollars per month on inventory for his small business. His credit card company offers 1-2% cash back, so he uses this to get Walmart gift cards. Every couple months he will give me a couple $100.00 gift cards, and I use these to buy groceries, gift items and anything else we might need. I realize that most people shouldn't be spending thousands of dollars every month on credit cards, but there are other programs that offer gift cards, and cards are often given away as prizes or all-purpose gifts. Larger chain grocery stores are more likely to have gift cards in circulation than smaller mom-and-pop stores.

2 . By using gift cards (received as gifts or through rewards programs) to make normal household purchases, it is income that you are not paying income tax on, which saves another 10-30% depending on your tax bracket.

3 . They have everything- not just groceries. Walmart Supercenters are a one stop shop, where we can buy everything from tortillas to toilet paper to batteries and sewing shears. This saves time and money spent on gas. Remember: the more time you spend shopping, the more money you spend.

4 . Price matching. Walmart will price match other stores. In fact, they even have a "Savings Catcher" app that will scan your receipts and give you a rebate if any items you have bought have lower prices at other stores.

If you could save $1000.00 per year by shopping at Walmart, and give that $1000.00 to an anti-abortion charity, wouldn't it outweigh the $10.00 of your yearly spending that might go to support abortion? If shopping at Walmart could help you quit your job to become a stay-at-home mom to your child, wouldn't that be more important than buying $5.00 bread at the farmers market, to support a local baker who bought all of HER ingredients at Walmart?

I am sure that some of our friends think my husband and I are low-class sell-outs because we only shop at Walmart. However, I don't really care because saving so much money at

Walmart helps us give money to charitable causes, buy local where it counts (the neighbor kid's lemonade stand or animals raised by 4-H kids) and live a life that we both absolutely love.

Warehouse Clubs: A Good Idea?

Many people think they are saving money by shopping at large warehouse clubs. Some of them probably do. However, keep in mind that you would have to save enough money using the warehouse to justify the $50.00 (or so) annual fee.

The bottom line for our family is that we don't buy enough groceries, and I'm good enough at finding deals without a warehouse club that it would be silly for us to join one. It is like paying $25.00 to have a store credit card that gives you 1% back. In order to make it worth the fee, you must spend at least $2500.00 at the store every year. If you spend less than that, you are paying $25.00 for nothing. Same thing with warehouse clubs.

A great alternative to warehouse clubs are restaurant supply stores. These require no membership (therefore, no fee), but still offer the same bulk discounts very consistently. We go to Gordon Food Service once every 3-6 months. This is where I buy a lot of my dairy products to shred and/or put in the freezer for the next several months. The mozzarella cheese is $2.00 per pound, and it freezes very well. There are a few other things we get at Gordon's, too.

Bent 'n' Dent Stores

For miscellaneous food purchases (dressings, baking supplies, and any kind of processed food), I like to shop at discount stores. At my house we call these stores "bent 'n' dents" because they sell food that is not good enough for the regular grocery stores. In our area this is a popular business for Amish and Mennonite folks, probably because refrigeration isn't required for such items.

Some people are too snooty to shop at discount stores. Many of the items are outdated, and such people think it is unsafe or unsanitary to eat something that is outdated. It's important to keep in mind though, that if a box says "sell by" "best by" or "best used by" and the date is expired, it is probably still safe to eat. For non-perishable items like baking mixes, spices or canned goods, an expiration date tells you when the item has passed its peak quality. The *quality* of these products might decline after the date, but they are still safe to eat. There is a reason why we call such foods "non-perishable". Unlike meat, eggs, dairy and produce, they don't really go bad.

Chocolate is an example of something that loses quality with age. After a year or so, it starts to taste different. However, the taste difference will be much less noticeable if the chocolate is used in baked goods. Nuts also lose quality as they age, but again you can disguise the taste in baked goods or by making nut butter. Stale chips or bread can be used in soup. These foods are still very safe to eat and they can provide nutrition and variety for pennies on the dollar.

Some of the prices I've found at the bent 'n' dent include dried cranberries for $2.40 per pound, quick oats for $0.75 per pound, Cliff bars for $0.07 per bar, tortillas for $0.35 per pound. and sliced ham for $1.39 per pound.

Dollar Tree Stores

At the Dollar Tree, everything is priced at $1.00. Many stores have non-perishable food items similar to what a bent 'n' dent would carry, although some Dollar Tree stores have meats and produce as well.

I have found that many items are 50% off what you would normally pay. Some people claim that, like bent 'n' dent stores, Dollar Tree food is expired. I am not sure if this is true, but as I've mentioned above, most non-perishable foods are still safe to eat after they've passed the "best by" date. I have noticed that some of the Dollar Tree foods do not taste as good, but I reckon they will not make you sick. Though some of the foods taste a little bit off, we have had a lot of Dollar Tree food that is just as good as Walmart; ice cream cones, windmill cookies, and Ramen noodles, to name a few.

On a recent trip to the Dollar Tree, I found pasta for $0.66 per pound (cheaper than I've found it at the bent 'n' dent), ice cream cones for $1.00 (a savings of $0.68), tortillas for $0.62 per pound less ($0.03 less per tortilla, but the Dollar Tree tortillas were also bigger), and sunflower seeds for $0.21 per pound less than retail. Ramen noodles were 5/$1.00, or $0.10 per package cheaper than at Walmart (though $0.05 per package more expensive than at the bent 'n' dent).

If you are looking for junk food, then the Dollar Tree is a good place to check. Popular kinds of cereal can be bought for $1.00 per (smallish) box. Cheese crackers, cookies, and other snack foods can be found for less as well, especially if you just need a small amount. Instead of buying a large box of cereal for $3.00, you can get a small one for $1.00. This can be especially helpful if you are on the beginner's budget and need a large variety of foods for a small amount of money. Don't forget that you can also use Ibotta rebates for "any brand" items like pasta. Using a $0.25 rebate on a $1.00 item is an automatic 25% off that item.

Sometimes the prices are so good at the Dollar Tree that I wonder if the product is legitimate. On my last trip, I bought almost a pound of Himalayan pink salt for $1.00. I checked all of the ingredients looking for pink food coloring or other tell-tale signs of fakeness, and I couldn't find anything. If the product truly was Himalayan pink salt, it was a steal of a deal and I should have bought ALL of the containers.

Bulk Food Stores

If you have them in your area (do a Google search), shopping at bulk food stores can save money on dry goods like beans, flour and rice. Some bulk food stores are health-oriented, while others are more like bent 'n' dent stores. Many Amish bulk stores I have been to offer candies, sprinkles, chocolate coating and other baking items at a good price. Make sure you double check your price book, though, to see if the bulk price is actually the most frugal option.

Produce Auctions

Depending on where you live, you may be able to find a wholesale produce auction and buy fresh fruits and vegetables in bulk. In our area there is a local Amish produce auction that is held a couple days per week during the summer months. Sometimes they sell by the box, crate, or pallet. If the quantities are too large, you can split the cost with a friend or neighbor. Again, double check you price book before buying a large quantity of anything.

If you don't live in Amish country, you may still be able to find markets or warehouse auctions that sell bulk amounts of produce for a very discounted price.

Shopping Challenge

Here are some things you can do this month to lower your grocery bill.

1. Use the free printable on my website to make your own price book, or download a price book app on your phone.

2. Make a price list (from information in your price book) and start comparing like food items by the pound. What is the cheapest fruit? What is the cheapest vegetable? Cheapest meat? Cheapest carbohydrate?

3. Buy meat in bulk. Pressure can or freeze what you cannot use right away.

4. Build a pantry where you can store your canned or frozen food.

5. Re-evaluate health priorities and determine "needs" from "wants".

6. Unsubscribe from any multi-level marketing plans you have signed up for.

7. Shop sales at a large chain grocery store.

8. Shop at a restaurant supply store.

9. Shop at a discount "bent 'n' dent" store.

10. Shop at a Dollar Tree.

11. Shop at a bulk food store.

12. Download a rebate app on your phone, and see if there are some "any brand" rebates that you can use.

13. Try using coupons. Sites like the Krazy Coupon Lady will help you match up deals so you won't have to spend any money.

Buying Individual Foods

Meat: Buying the Cut or the Entire Animal?

Some of you may be wondering if it is more frugal to buy an entire cow for beef, say, than just buying the separate cuts of meat at the grocery store (or farmers market, or wherever you buy meat).

If you are interested in buying grass fed or other specially raised meats, it may be better to buy a whole or half animal. Keep in mind though that some animals are sold by their live weight, which includes the fur, skin, bones and other non-edible parts. Other animals are sold by "hanging weight"; how much the animal weighs at the butcher when the head, feet, organs, hide and blood are removed. This weight still includes the bones and a lot of other non-edible parts, and you might get 60% of the hanging weight back in actual meat. If you pay $2.00/lb. hanging weight for a beef cow, as an example, you will be paying more like $3.33/lb. for the actual meat. This price, then, is for ALL of the meat you get, from sirloin to stew meat.

Hanging/live weight to finished meat per animal:
Beef: 60% take home (hanging weight)
Lamb: 51% take home (live weight)
Pork: 84% take home (16% atypical cuts- organs, hocks, etc.) (hanging weight)

If you just want to buy supermarket quality meats, I would say it is a better deal to buy single cuts. Why? Because when you purchase a whole animal, the price of the more expensive cuts- for example, filet minion- are factored into the price of the animal along with the cheaper cuts like ground beef or chuck roast. If you are trying to save money, you ONLY want the cheap cuts. Plus, if you purchase a whole animal there will probably be several pieces of meat that will go to waste because you don't know how to cook them, or don't like them.

Rationing Meat

Meat is often the costliest element of a meal. One way to curb meat spending is to only serve a single portion of meat, per person, per meal. If you do this, make sure there are plenty of other appetizing sides that people can have unlimited amounts of. Bread or beans are good fillers to serve after the main dish.

The other day I decided to make brats for lunch. There were only three brats left in the package, and I knew that wouldn't fill up my hungry, hardworking husband, let alone both of us. So I added sides of cheesy potatoes, corn chips and a large salad. We finished off the brats and potatoes, but there were still plenty of corn chips and salad left. Even though the meat was technically rationed, we both thoroughly enjoyed the main course as well as the other sides.

Finding Free Meat

We eat a lot of meat compared to many frugal families, but that is because we get most of it for free. Some of it is gifted to us or bartered (namely pork and beef). We raise our own chickens, and harvest venison whenever possible, by hunting or processing a deer that has been hit by a car.

To get road-kill venison, have the policeman bring you a deer tag when he comes out to see the car. You don't have to be the one who hit the deer in order to harvest it. That would be expensive! Not many people want to go through the work to butcher a maimed deer, so if a friend or family member has hit one, it is worth asking if they are going to keep the meat. One time we heard that someone had hit a deer around the corner from our house. We drove down to check it out. The car wasn't there anymore, but the police vehicle was. My husband walked over and asked the police lady if the other people wanted the meat and how long ago it had been hit. The deer had been hit within the hour and the car owners didn't want it, so she gave us a tag and we were able to salvage about 10 pounds of meat when we got home. For free!

Our chicken supply is also free. Instead of buying broiler chicks and raising them for six weeks on broiler feed, we harvest the roosters and old hens from our laying flock. We have also had roosters and chickens given to us, and we've found roosters for free on Craigslist. There is a fair amount of meat on some of these chickens, and others probably aren't worth butchering, but it IS free meat. If you are hurting for money and not getting enough protein in your diet, all you need is a boning knife and a pot of boiling water to butcher a free chicken. There are plenty of tutorials on Youtube and different blogs that will show you how to butcher a chicken.

The one common denominator with all of our free meat is that we do the butchering ourselves. It will be well worth your time to learn how to process poultry and small game, if nothing else. When people know that you are knowledgeable and willing to butcher, they are more likely to tell you about injured chickens, roadkill deer, and other opportunities for free or cheap meat. Or perhaps they would be willing to share some of the meat with you if you help with butchering.

Beef: For our first year of marriage, we simply didn't eat beef unless it was given to us; there was plenty of ground venison in the freezer to use instead. When we ran out of venison, though, I did start buying large 20 lb. logs of ground beef at the store. This meat cost about $2.50 per pound, which is a reasonable price for beef. When I got the log home, I would freeze it in one pound packages to be used later.

Last year, a family member got out of the dairy business and asked us to help process their last cow. As a thank-you gift, they gave us enough ground beef to fill part of our freezer with. Wow! Technically, this meat was free to us. All it cost was a day of our time (and we spent the rest of that day butchering a lamb of ours, so we had the equipment out anyway). As opposed to the store bought beef, this meat was leaner and grass-fed. It goes to show that sometimes cheaper really is better.

Poultry: During the summer of 2014, I tried raising meat chickens. This worked out okay, but after buying the broiler chicks and broiler feed, our birds ended up costing about $1.00 per pound. You can get chicken from the store for $0.75 per pound, and cheaper than that when it goes on sale. For all the work involved, and the fact that our chickens weren't even being fed organically, I decided not to raise broilers again.

During the next year, I simply bought big bags of chicken legs at the store for $0.60 per pound, and froze or pressure canned them. This is a good, dependable way to buy cheap meat regularly.

Last year, we were blessed to be given an entire flock (30+) of laying hens. The hens were various ages. We were also given a broody hen with chicks, five ISA Brown pullets, and several roosters from other people. We ended up butchering a lot of the roosters, keeping the best for breeding. We will also start butchering some of the older, non-laying hens when we run out of meat in the freezer or pantry. This meat is completely free for us, apart from the time taken to process it (my husband and I can do five or six birds in about two hours... we are not the fastest).

Turkey goes on sale around Thanksgiving. Some people use those sales to stock up on turkeys for the year. You can also buy frozen boneless turkey roasts, thaw, and use a meat slicer to cut the roast into thin slices. Then re-freeze the slices and use as lunchmeat throughout the year. I bought my meat slicer at a garage sale for $5.00, but if you don't have one you can ask the butcher at your grocery store to cut your roast into slices for you. I have been told that they will do it for free.

Pork: To be honest, we don't eat much pork. What we do eat has been gifted to us by friends and family, bartered with pork-raising neighbors, or purchased on sale at the grocery store. Though we don't eat pork chops or ground pork regularly, I do use a small amount of ham, bacon or sausage on things like pizza or scrambled eggs. I have found sliced ham at the bent 'n' dent grocery store for $1.39 per pound, and sausage at $0.59 per pound. When you find deals like this, it's good to stock up. When the sausage I found was hot and spicy, I simply mixed it half and half with regular ground beef. The end result was excellent in potato hash and soups.

Ham often goes on sale during Christmas, Thanksgiving and Easter. Like frozen turkey roasts, you can also use a meat cutter to process boneless hams into sliced ham and use this as lunch meat.

Fish: Again, fish is one of those things we just don't eat. Early on in our marriage I would purchase fish every week for a Friday meal, and then I realized that I was spending $5.00 per week on this one meal. I knew we would enjoy hamburgers just as much (and our ground venison was practically free, unlike the fish), so I stopped buying fish. Now we eat fish when it's been given to us or if we've gone fishing (which is... never. Although there is a pond back behind our property, so it's possible). I also enjoy ordering fish at restaurants because we don't eat it at home.

Other: Other meats that we have had in our freezer before are lamb and goat meat (chevon). The lamb was one that we had bought at a 4-H livestock sale. I had got the lamb with intentions of breeding and having my own sheep farm, but that didn't work out. So the lamb ended up in the freezer.

We also have goat meat in the freezer sometimes because I keep dairy goats. Now and then we have a buck/wether (wethers are castrated males) born that we don't need on our farm, and so we keep him until he is full grown to butcher.

When we have the opportunity to get "random" meats like goat and lamb, it is usually my husband and I doing the processing. We put about two thirds of the animal into ground meat (more versatile and easy to use) and the other third is cut into steaks and roasts. Little scrap pieces are cut into chunks and canned that way; excellent when used for tacos or fajitas. We try to remove as much of the fat as possible, because it taints the flavor of the meat and also because I use it to make soap. If you are canning meat, the fat will often rise to the top of the jar and solidify during storage. This rendered fat can be peeled off and also used for cooking or making soap.

Eggs: Eggs are one of the most nutritious foods to have on hand. I try to have eggs for breakfast (about two eggs per person) as often as possible. Though perhaps more expensive than oatmeal or hot cereal, eggs are still more nutritious and filling. Plus cleanup is a lot easier if you are feeding young children. Adding a little bit of onion, green pepper, salsa, bacon, ham, or a sprinkle of shredded cheese will make scrambled eggs more exciting. If served with sour cream and tortillas, "doctored" scrambled eggs can be used for an entire meal.

Egg prices can fluctuate wildly. I remember one week not being able to find any eggs (of any size) for less than $2.29, and a few weeks later there were large eggs for sale at $1.60 per dozen. Recently I have seen eggs on sale for as little as $0.69 per dozen.

Eggs are one item you <u>need</u> to have in your price book. Then you will be able to predict when they will go on sale and how much you should or shouldn't pay for a dozen.

When you do find some eggs on sale, be sure to stock up. Most people refrigerate eggs and therefore are less likely to buy a lot at one time. However, eggs will last four to six weeks in a cool place (like a basement) without any refrigeration at all. If you want to store eggs for more than a couple weeks, they can be frozen. Just separate the whites and yolks, and freeze the yolks in one bag/container and the whites in another.

As I've written before, we eat eggs for free because I have chickens. I sell enough eggs to pay for the feed, and we eat the cracked or small eggs that are left over.

Dairy

Below are some of my best tips for saving money on dairy.

For Beginners: How to Split a Gallon of Milk

Those of you on the beginner's budget ($20.00 per week) may be wondering where all of the dairy is going to come from when you can only afford a gallon of milk and nothing else every week. The answer lies in good cooking skills!

1. **Use one and a half quarts of the milk to make cheese** with vinegar, salt and Italian herbs. This amount of milk will make over 1/4 lb. of cheese. You can read about how to do this on my blog (www.therenaissancehousewife.com).

2. **Use one and a half quarts of milk to make yogurt** (see recipe below). The yogurt can be used for eating, but also for making yogurt cheese (like cream cheese) or strained into Greek yogurt for salad dressing.

3. **Use one quart of milk for drinking, baking** or making smoothies ("ice cream") with.

On a bare-bones budget, there is not enough money for things like butter or sour cream. Thankfully, sour cream is not a necessity and other animal fats besides butter can be used for cooking. When you have started gardening or finding free produce and meat, then you can start spending more of the budget on dairy products.

Milk: I did not grow up drinking milk. Today, neither my husband nor I drink milk as a beverage so we do not go through a lot of it. I tend to think it is a waste for adults to drink milk when they could be drinking water and getting more nutrition from dairy products like yogurt or cheese.

At this point in time, I have one Nigerian Dwarf milking goat that supplies us with milk. She gives between one pint and seven cups per day (more just after kidding, and less toward the end of the season), six months out of the year, which is enough to make yogurt, as well as some cheese and butter when there is extra. The cost to keep her (grain & hay- not including breeding) averages out to $11.00 per month. I cover this cost by selling her kids and goat's milk soap. If I were not selling things, our cost per gallon would be about $3.47. At this time grocery store milk is about $2.50, but then again grocery store milk isn't fresh or unpasteurized. Goat milk at the store is about $16.00 per gallon, so if you want goat milk or raw milk, keeping your own goat is a great deal. The Nigerian Dwarf breed is small and friendly. Our goat is so easy to handle, she is like our family dog.

Like eggs, milk prices will fluctuate wildly depending on the year. Be sure to keep track of them in your price book.

Cheese: We buy our cheese at a restaurant supply

company. Mozzarella cheese is $2.00 per pound, and shredded cheddar cheese costs about $2.50 per pound. The little one-pound packages at the grocery store are TWICE that price. In addition to hard cheese, we also buy cream cheese at the same store for just under $2.00 per pound.

Cottage cheese doesn't freeze particularly well, so I only buy that with a coupon or if it is on sale. It is possible to freeze, but the flavor and texture gets altered, making it suitable only for things like casseroles or lasagna. I use goat cheese for these purposes, so I don't buy cottage cheese to freeze. However, it reportedly lasts longer if stored upside down in the fridge.

Butter: We also buy butter at the restaurant supply store or when it goes on sale. If I run out and need to buy butter at the grocery store, I get the two-pound packages because they are available at a slight discount.

Recently I have started making my own butter with goat's milk. You can read more about this in the "fats and oils" section.

Yogurt: I've gotten into the habit of making my own yogurt. It is a fraction of the cost of store bought, and simple to make.

1. Heat 2 quarts of milk to 180 degrees Fahrenheit.
2. Let the milk cool to between 105-115 degrees Fahrenheit.
3. Stir in one small snack-size container of yogurt

(containing active live cultures).

4. Pour mixture into yogurt maker or mason jars. If using a yogurt maker, follow the instructions that came with it. If using jars, fill a cooler most of the way full with hot, hot tap water. Set the jars inside the cooler (so they are surrounded by hot water) and top off the cooler with a kettle full of <u>boiling</u> water. Put the lid on the cooler.

5. Let the yogurt incubate for 8-12 hours.

6. Dry off the yogurt container/jars and refrigerate until use.

You can find more information about making yogurt on the "Recipes" page at www.therenaissancehousewife.com.

Sour Cream: We have a lot of Mexican-style food at our house, so I buy sour cream on a weekly or bi-weekly basis, without coupons or sales. Unfortunately this, like cottage cheese, does not freeze well, so I can't stockpile when there IS a sale. However, there is a very good off-brand of sour cream called "Monticello" that I buy. It costs 30-40% less than name brands and only contains cream and enzyme (no fillers like guar gum or preservatives). It costs $1.28 per pound, and if I'm careful, I can make a single container last for two weeks.

Ice Cream: I would love to say that it is frugal to make your own ice cream, but unfortunately it is actually more expensive to make unless you have some free cream to use. Buying heavy cream at the store is very costly, so if you want to indulge in this sweet treat, you are almost better off to purchase an off-brand variety or buy it on sale. In our area we pay $2.50-$3.00 for a 1.75 quart container. Be careful when comparing ice cream prices: some brands come in 1.5 quart boxes.

The good news about buying ice cream at the grocery store is that it is much, much cheaper than going to an ice cream shop! When it was hot this summer, we found ourselves at the ice cream shop at least once a week (because I refused to keep ice cream at home for health reasons). My husband finally convinced me that we could buy a whole box of ice cream for the price of a single cone. In fact, if neither of us got a cone, we could use the money to buy two different kinds of ice cream AND a box of waffle cones. I am a sucker for waffle cones, so that is what we did. I doubt that we will buy ice cream during the cooler months, but as an alternative to buying at the ice cream shop, buying ice cream at the store is very frugal.

Tip: you can find the cheapest sugar cones at the Dollar Tree. We did a taste test, and they were almost identical in flavor to the name brand cones.

If you are really dead set against buying ice cream at the store, you can always make a "milk ice" dessert, or a fruit-based frozen dessert, that kind of tastes like ice cream if you use your imagination. I make these for pennies using a banana, strawberries, yogurt or milk, and a little bit of sugar for sweetener.

Vegetables

Spend $0.00 on Produce: Learn to Garden

The first and most obvious suggestion I have for saving money in the produce aisle is, of course, to not shop there at all. Everyone should at least *try* gardening before they decide that they hate it and it's too much work.

Instead of planning an enormous garden filled with everything in the seed catalog, start small. I would highly recommend starting with one raised bed and one or two types of vegetables. Build your raised bed in the autumn. Fill it with alternating layers of grass clippings, dead leaves and animal manure. Get out the hose and soak the entire bed with water. Cover the bed with cardboard or newspaper, and put a pallet or two on top to hold everything in place. This will decompose over the winter and turn into a rich bed of compost for your plants.

When spring time rolls around, go to the local nursery and buy a couple of cheap $0.50 plants (tomato or bell pepper are good choices). Remove the pallet from your raised bed and punch holes in the cardboard where you want your plants to be. Plant each one and give it a good watering.

Depending on the state of your cardboard or newspaper in the spring, you may or may not have to mulch the bed with grass clippings. If weeds start to come up, pull them and put more mulch on. For the rest of the summer you should only have to spend a few minutes every week weeding, watering, picking off bugs or pruning the plants (if you grow tomatoes). Trust me, gardening should NOT be time consuming or hard!

If you are ambitious, plant some perennial herbs (sage, lavender, mint, chives, etc.) or a patch of raspberries or strawberries. Fresh herbs and fruit are more expensive to buy at the store, so they are more worth your time than potatoes, carrots or even green beans.

I measure the success of my garden not by how pretty it looks, but how much free food I get for the hours of work I put in. Sometimes I can sell the extras at a farmers market and even *make* money from my garden.

Buying Fresh Produce in Bulk

Depending on where you live, you may be able to find a fresh produce market or auction where fruits and vegetables are heavily discounted. Make sure the bulk produce is actually cheaper before you buy. A good plan of action is to eat all that you can fresh, and then preserve the rest by canning, freezing, drying or fermenting for your pantry. If there is still too much, split the bounty with a friend.

Potatoes: Every year I watch my mother-in-law's potato patch get eaten alive by bugs, despite "dusting" and fearless attempts to collect and destroy the little pests. Of course she still gets a lot of free potatoes despite the bugs, but it looks like a lot of work to me. This is when I'm happy that grocery stores offer such huge bags of potatoes for a relatively good price. Maybe someday I will grow my own potatoes, but probably not any time soon.

Potatoes typically go on sale during Thanksgiving. You can load up at that time, and stretch the bounty for several months. Potatoes will keep from 3-5 weeks in the pantry and 3-4 months in the fridge. They can also be shredded and frozen (think hash browns!) or pressure canned if you want them to last even longer. I actually "shred" my potatoes in the blender (if you don't have a high-end blender, you can probably do the same thing with a food processor). Peeled potato quarters are put in the container and covered with water. Then I turn it on for 10 seconds or so, and pour the water/potato mixture into a colander, where all of the water drains and I am left with little potato "shreds".

Potatoes are my go-to starch when cooking because they are typically cheaper than pasta or rice (though we do have those items to eat as well). Potatoes are a good starch to use in meals if you are trying to be gluten free.

Tomatoes: I don't usually buy fresh tomatoes. On occasion I will have a $0.25 Ibotta rebate for tomatoes and buy one Roma tomato (with the rebate, the tomato is free) to use in tacos. Otherwise I will use garden tomatoes for tacos and sandwiches, or we will find other things to have with our meals. I think fresh tomatoes are nice, but not really a necessity.

Every year I plant a lot of tomatoes for canning. Instead of canning the tomatoes whole, I put them in the blender and use the puree as a base for enchilada sauce (basically an all-purpose tomato sauce for Mexican dishes) and marinara sauce (an all-purpose sauce for Italian dishes). I have also done ketchup and other sauces in the past, but enchilada and marinara get used the most. If I have extra tomatoes and peppers, I will make salsa to can as well. In the past I have canned tomato juice (to use in chili or soups), but it is more work and takes more storage space than tomato paste/sauce, which can be used for the exact same purposes.

In 2016, I was short on time for canning. Instead of making two different sauces, I just made one all-purpose, non-flavored tomato sauce. First I blended the raw tomatoes, then let the juice sit overnight in the fridge. When the puree and water had separated, I ladled the puree off the top into a saucepan, and discarded the water. Then I cooked the puree down a bit before canning in pint jars (if you don't cook the puree, it will separate again; the pulp on top, and water on the bottom). I will have to add the appropriate spices to this sauce when I am ready to use it.

When I buy a tomato product from the store, it is usually tomato paste. You can thin the paste out with water to make tomato soup, chili, or other tomato-based meals to whatever consistency you want. Because it's a canned product, I've also found tomato paste at discount stores for very, very cheap. It's a great pantry item to have on hand in replacement of fresh tomatoes.

Carrots: Carrots are rather easy to grow, but they are also cheap to buy at the store. They are full of nutrition and a great vegetable to cook with during the winter months. You can cut larger carrots into sticks for snacking, instead of buying baby carrots, in order to save money. Another way to save is by purchasing bulk carrots instead of carrots that have been bagged already. Sometimes I find sales or rebates on carrots, which is helpful for an item I'm going to buy anyway. If you find an absolute bargain and want to stock up on carrots, they can be frozen or pressure canned. Carrots will also keep unrefrigerated for several months if they are packed in sand inside a plastic storage tub. Make sure the carrots aren't touching each other, and keep the tub in a cool place (such as a garage or basement).

Onions: You can grow your own onions and it is cheaper than buying them, but as a fledgling gardener, I still prefer to buy them on a monthly basis. That way I don't have to worry about home-grown onions going bad in the pantry, or use valuable freezer space to store them.

I planted an experimental patch of onions from sets this year. The packet of onion sets cost $1.86, and I harvested 4.7 lbs. of onions. The value of the onions minus $1.86 was only $2.04; a paltry savings for the work involved. Growing onions may be in my future, but only if I can grow them from seed (more plants for less money) and if they store well. If not, I will be happy to continue buying them at the grocery store for $0.83 per pound.

Recently I was given a couple of onions that had rotted in one spot. Instead of throwing out all of the onions, I simply cut out the molded spot and threw the other 3/4 of the onion into the blender to be chopped up. After chopping, I froze the onion so it wouldn't continue to go bad in the fridge.

Celery: Celery is cheap at the store, and usually a bargain for the money. It can also be frozen if you find a deal and want to stockpile. Unfortunately celery is hard to grow here in Michigan, so I tend to choose other veggies for snacking and cooking. If you don't have a garden, however, celery is a good deal for the money. You can also use it to replace more-expensive bell peppers in certain recipes.

One time I had only a few sticks of celery left. My husband had declared that he wouldn't eat it and it was too limp for my tastes, so I diced it up into small pieces and put it in the dehydrator. The celery kept its flavor VERY well, so I used it in soups.

Bell peppers: These have become very pricey in the last few years. Even plain old green peppers are almost $1.00 each at the grocery store. Like lettuce, my rule on peppers is to never buy them at the store. Instead, I grow a whole raised bed or two in my garden, and then slice/dice and freeze them for use during the winter. We do have some fresh peppers in the summer, but otherwise we only eat frozen peppers in stir fry or fajita-type meals.

If I really HAD to buy bell peppers (to serve at a baby or bridal shower, for example), I'd go to my favorite restaurant supply store and buy a bag of three to nine peppers. Then after making my vegetable tray, I'd cut up what was left over and put it in the freezer for fajitas or pizza topping.

Lettuce: Using a cold frame, we are able to have free lettuce for nine months out of the year. During the summer there is a great abundance (I make a lot of salads during this time!), but in the spring and fall there may only be enough for sandwiches or tacos. That is okay. My rule is to never buy lettuce, and when I don't have it, to just cook with other vegetables that are cheap or in season.

During the summer when I use lettuce for salads, I go out to the garden and cut enough heads for a whole week. When I bring them inside, I break off all of the leaves and soak them in a bowl of cold water. Then break the leaves into smaller pieces and put them in a salad spinner. After spinning once, I add more water (to loosen leftover bugs or dirt), drain, and spin once more. After draining the few drops of water collected from the second spin, I still spin the lettuce one final time. Then I pile the pieces of the lettuce onto a clean dish towel. The lettuce pieces are rolled up in the towel and placed in a plastic bag. This is put into the crisper drawer of the refrigerator, where the lettuce will keep for at least a week. That way when I decide to serve lettuce, it is washed, cut and ready to go.

Did you know that you can grow **green onions** on your window sill? Save the white, fleshy root parts and put them in a glass of water. In a week or two, the tops will grow back! You can cut the tops for weeks before the water starts to get old and decompose the roots.

If you really enjoy making salads during the winter, consider using **cabbage** instead of iceberg lettuce. It is a lot more nutritious and cheaper than any kind of lettuce per pound.

Another alternative to salad greens are **sprouts**. You can make your own sprouts with lentils, wheat berries, amaranth, (unhulled) barley, buckwheat, corn, einkorn, farro, kamut, millet, whole oats, quinoa, rice, rye berries, sorghum, spelt and other legumes or grains. Just put 1/4 cup of seeds in a quart jar. Soak the seeds in water for 12 hours (or overnight), and afterward drain the water. Then every day, rinse the seeds in water by submersing them and pouring off the water. You do not have to submerse them for a long time- just enough to get them all wet. In a few days, you will notice the seeds beginning to sprout. You can keep watering the seeds for a few days after that, and they will grow enough to fill up the jar. You will want to refrigerate the sprouts before they start to mold, though. Once refrigerated, the sprouts will last from three to seven days. You can use sprouts in salads, or like lettuce in soups, sandwiches and wraps.

Free Vegetables: Foraging

Another way to acquire free vegetables without the hassle

of gardening is to learn about edible plants in your area. Greens and other wild vegetables are plentiful in nature and easy to harvest. Many can be used in salads, soups, sandwiches, or even made into pickles. Below are 28 wild vegetables to put on your foraging list.

Arrowhead (*Sagittaria*): Roots can be cooked and eaten like potatoes. Was a favorite of Lewis and Clark on their journeys.

Burdock (*Arctium*): Roots can be eaten, as well as young leaf stems and leaves. Most parts will need to be peeled and boiled.

Cattail (*Typha*): Roots and lower shoots can be eaten, as well as the young shoots. The greenish-yellow flower spikes can be husked like corn and boiled before being eaten, and lastly, the pollen can be shaken off and used as a flour extender.

Chickory (*Chichorium*): Greens can be eaten.

Chufa (*Cyperus*): Roots can be washed and eaten raw, or cooked.

Clover (*Trifolium*): All parts of this plant were historically eaten by Native Americans, and we can do the same.

Chickweed (*Stellaria*) (*Alsine*): This is one of my favorite wild greens. It has a bland taste and is available much of the year.

Dandelion (*Taraxacum*): Roots, crowns (white part between the root and surface of the ground), leaves and flower buds are all edible. Younger leaves are less bitter than the older ones, but even the mature leaves can be mellowed by boiling in water.

Dock (*Rumex*): Leaves can be fried with a little salt and butter before being eaten. If too bitter, the leaves can be boiled. The stem of this plant has also been used as an alternative to rhubarb.

Glasswort (*Salicornia*)- Stems can be made into pickles. It can also be used raw for salads or cooked.

Wild Grape (*Vitis*): Leaves can be used for making stuffed wild grape leaves.

Green Amaranth (*Amaranthus*): Young greens can be used fresh or cooked as any other green. They are better before they go to seed.

Jerusalem Artichoke (*Helianthus*): Roots can be used as potatoes. They can also be turned into pickles, pies, or eaten raw.

Knotweed (*Polygonum*): Roots can be roasted or boiled; young stems can be cooked like asparagus, used in salad, or the older stems can be peeled and cooked like rhubarb.

Lambsquarter (*Chenopodium*): This plant was widely used by American Indians. The flavor is mild, which is why it is one of my favorites. You can boil, sautee or eat the greens raw.

Milkweed (*Asclepias*): Tender young sprouts up to 8" high can be cooked (boiled) and eaten like asparagus. The buds and leaves are also edible, as long as they have been boiled to neutralize the bitter milky sap.

Miner's Lettuce (*Montia*): This plant was named for those men who participated in the gold rush of 1849. The Native Americans showed them how to use greens like this to prevent scurvy and other nutritional deficiencies. As many other wild greens, this one becomes bitter with age but can be boiled to improve the flavor.

Wild Mustard (*Brassica*): Young greens are edible. They may require more quantity and a longer boiling time than other plants (30 minutes or more). The flowers can be eaten like broccoli after being simmered for a few minutes.

Nettles (*Urtica*): Typically considered too painful to touch, nettles can be gathered with gloves and then dropped in boiling water to quell the bristles (dried nettles can be made into tea). Only use new growth on the plant. Nettles contain a lot of minerals and are one of the best flavored wild greens as well.

Plantain (*Plantago*): Leaves can be eaten raw when young, and cooked later like spinach.

Pokeweed (*Phytolacca*): Young pokeweed shoots (no more than 8" tall) can be cooked and eaten like asparagus. One of my books even tells how you can "force" this plant in your basement and have greens throughout the winter!

Purslane (*Portulaca*): Purslane should be well washed because it grows low to the ground. It can be used raw, cooked, pickled, or even frozen. It helps give body to soups and stews. Purslane is normal fare for many immigrants from the Middle East (see the Flavor Family index).

Salsify (*Tragopogon*): Roots can be scraped and cooked like turnips while young. The young leaves, root crown and stems are also edible.

Shepherd's Purse (*Capsella*): Leaves can be used in salad or cooked.

Toothwort (*Dentaria*): Roots can be chopped and added to sandwiches or salads.

Watercress (*Nasturtium*): Stems, leaves, flowers and young pods can be cooked and eaten. Because watercress naturally grows in water, it is smart to boil the greens to eliminate any chance of contamination.

Wild Lettuce (*Lactuca*): Can be cooked and used in the same way as dandelion. Eat it before the plant is 16" tall.

Wintercress (*Barbarea*): Pick greens before they blossom, or after the first fall frost. They can be boiled once or twice (depending on how bitter they were to begin with). The buds can also be cooked as you would broccoli.

Fruits

It's a popular practice to serve whole fruits as a snack. However, as the oldest of nine children, I saw PLENTY of good fruit go to waste when a toddler or small child took a couple bites and decided he was done eating. Instead of giving each person a whole fruit, cut each piece in half, or even in smaller sections for more expensive fruit. If kids are still hungry, you can always give them the other half of the apple. But nobody will want to *finish* a half-eaten and drooled-on apple.

Preserving Fruit

Many fruits are acidic, and are easily preserved using a water bath canner. Most of them can be made into jams, jellies, sauces, or just canned as-is. Surplus fruit can also be made into wine, which is a good way to save money. If you don't drink alcohol, the wine can still be used for marinating, cooking, or further fermented into vinegar.

Apples: Apples come into season during the fall. Depending on your area, you may be able to glean or forage apples. When I was growing up, it wasn't unusual to go pick apples at the home of a friend or neighbor who didn't want them. One season an orchard owner told us that we could pick off one of the back areas that hadn't been sprayed. They couldn't use the apples because they were "wormy", but we didn't want sprayed apples anyway. It was a perfect fit. Sometimes an orchard will also sell "drops".

If you do find apples on sale (or for free) in vast quantities, there are several things you can do to preserve them. 1) Make applesauce and can it, 2) dry thin slices to make apple chips, or 3) make apple pie filling to can. If you don't like the "canned pie filling" pies, you can always just freeze the spiced and sugared apple slices, or make pies with fresh apples and freeze them before they've been baked. Note: Unfortunately apple slices don't freeze well on their own, so unless you intend to use them frozen (as in smoothies) or cooked somehow, use drying or canning as a method of preservation.

Bananas: I like to buy "ripe" (brown or spotted) bananas on sale, and then freeze them (after they've been peeled) to use in smoothies. If you do buy and eat fresh bananas though, store them in a closed plastic bag to last longer.

For those of you who don't eat processed sugar, look into using bananas as a substitute in baking or pudding/dessert recipes. In some cases, bananas are much cheaper than sugar alternatives.

Lastly, if you are comparing the price of fruit per pound, keep in mind that around 33% of a banana's weight is the peel. This means that the price per pound of actual fruit is 50% higher than what is listed. For example, the true price of $0.50/lb. bananas is actually $0.75/lb., without the peel. Make sure you take this into account when comparing the price of bananas to other fruits (such as apples or strawberries) that don't have so much waste.

Oranges and Citrus Fruits: These typically go on sale during the winter months. Hint: If you need just a little bit of fresh lemon juice, don't cut the whole fruit in half. Prick it with a toothpick, squeeze out what you need and then replace the toothpick. The lemon will keep a lot longer that way.

Berries: Oftentimes berries are much cheaper to buy frozen than fresh. But before you go out and buy berries, check around to see if there are any wild berries you can forage on your own (or your neighbor's) property. Berries are very common in the wild.

You can also grow berries, be they strawberries, raspberries, or other berries, fairly easy in your own garden. Make sure to keep them mulched. Besides weeding, the only problem I have had with my berries is keeping the Japanese beetles off. Here is a good organic method for dealing with them; early in the morning, go out with a bowl of water with some dish soap mixed in. Drop the bugs into the water and they will die. Chickens especially love these beetles- a frugal treat for my feathered friends.

Peaches: Peach trees are relatively difficult to grow yourself, but you can buy peaches at a discount at the end of July. It may be cheaper to buy already canned or frozen peaches than to buy fresh ones and preserve them yourself.

Pears: Pears come into season in early September. If you can find a source of free pears, then by all means can them. I have not heard of anyone freezing pears, but I have heard of people making "pear sauce". Pear sauce is okay, but sometimes it can be gritty. As with peaches, it might be more frugal to buy pears already canned (on sale) than to buy fresh ones to can yourself.

Grapes: Sometimes grapes go on sale. When they do, you can either buy enough to eat fresh or buy some additional packages to freeze. Frozen grapes (cut them in half before you freeze them) are an interesting snack for children.

If you have a grape vine or know someone who does, there is nothing quite like fresh grapes in the autumn. Most homegrown grapes have seeds, but I just swallow the little fruits whole. Homegrown grapes can be also be made into grape juice.

Other Fruits: Generally I only buy other fruits when they are steeply discounted or on special occasions.

Free Fruits: Foraging

There are many fruits growing in the wild that you can harvest for freezing or to make jams, jellies, or wine with. Below, I have listed 20 such fruits. As you can imagine, there is hardly any reason to buy fruit for condiments or beverages when there is such a bounty available for free in the wild. As with any foraging, make sure you do your homework in order to properly identify each plant. The scope of this book is not long enough to provide recipes for each fruit, but you can find these resources at your local library or online.

Barberry (*Berberis*): Use to make drinks, tart sauces, jams, purees, and preserves. Berries can also be candied or pickled in vinegar.

Wild Blueberries (*Vaccinium*) (*Gaylussacia*): Use to make preserves. You can also freeze or dry the berries.

Buffalo Berry (*Shepherdia*): Sour, but rich in pectin. Use to make jelly. After a frost, the fruits are sweeter and can be eaten raw or cooked.

Chokecherry (*Prunus*): Use to make wine or jelly. If making jelly, and additional source of pectin is needed. Also, do not eat the pits; as all cherry pits, they are poisonous.

Wild and/or Highbush Cranberry (*Vaccinium*): Harvest after the first frost of autumn. Berries can be frozen or dried. Dried berries can be crushed into a dry powder and then reconstituted by simmering in water and adding sugar to taste.

Currants & Gooseberries (*Ribes*): Use to make pies, tarts, sauces, jams, jellies and wine.

Elderberry (*Sambucus*): Use dried or cooked, with sweeter berries for a better taste. Can be used to make jellies (add pectin), sauces, and wine. The flowers can be added to pancakes, muffins and fritters to add flavor.

Wild Grape (*Vitis*): Fruit, leaves and shoots are edible, but the roots are poisonous.   Use fruit to make jelly, conserves and pie. The leaves can be used in Middle Eastern cooking, gathered in the springtime while still tender and bottled in a saturated salt solution for use as you need them. Stuffed wild grape leaves are a good dish to try.

Ground Cherries (*Physalis*): Eat raw or use to make pies, sauces, preserves and jams.

May Apple (*Popophyllum*): Use the fruits to make jams and marmalades. The root, leaves and stem are poisonous.

Mountain Ash Berries (*Sorbus*): Use to make jams, jellies, and marmalades, or to flavor wine.

Mulberries (*Morus*): Use to make pies, jellies, and wines. Hot mulberries can be cooked with dumplings. Mulberry juice can be chilled to make a good summer drink. All mulberry recipes will benefit from a dash of lemon juice to balance their sweetness.

Pin Cherry (*Prunus*): Used to make jelly or syrup for pancakes.

Raspberry & Blackberry (*Rubus*): Freeze to use in baking or smoothies, as you would blueberries. Can also be used in cordials and wines. A nice raspberry shrub can be made by letting the fruit stand in vinegar for a month, then straining, sweetening to taste and diluting with ice water.

Rose Hips (*Rosa*): Use for jams, jellies and syrups.

Rum Cherry (*Prunus*): Also called wild cherry, this fruit can be used made a combination apple/cherry jelly, or can be jelly on their own with added pectin. Can also be made into sauces, pies, sherbets, and flavoring juices. Historically, the simmered and sweetened juice was added to raw liquors to smooth and stretch them. As with any cherry, the pit is poisonous so don't eat it.

Serviceberry (*Amelanchier*): Use in pies, muffins, pancakes, jams, jellies, sauces, preserves and wines.

Wild Strawberry (*Fragaria*): Use the leaves to make tea, or the fruits to make shortcakes, tarts, sauces, jellies, jams and preserves.

Wild Apple (*Malus*) (*Pyrus*): Used historically by Iroquois Indians to make applesauces sweetened with maple syrup.

Wild Plum (*Prunus*): Use to make jellies and jams, and some fruit can be eaten raw. Used historically by American colonists to mellow gin.

Grains & Beans

Grains and beans can often be purchased at a 50% discount simply by buying in bulk. I buy 10 lb. bags of white rice at Walmart. By doing this, I can get the rice for $0.45 per pound as opposed to $1.00. The same can be true for beans.

Beans: Sometimes you can also find great rice and bean deals at discount stores. During a recent trip to the Amish store, I found black beans AND white rice for $0.25 per pound. Of course, they only had one pound of black beans and two pounds of rice at that price, but I bought it anyway. After eating navy beans for the last nine months (because they are the cheapest... black beans are consistently more expensive) I was ready for a change.

Most of the time, it is cheaper to can your own beans. When you buy a 15 oz. can of beans, you are really buying about 3/4 cup of dried beans with 3/4 cup of water. If the can of beans costs $1.50, and the price of home-canned beans is $0.35 (3/4 cup of dry beans + $0.15 for new lid and heating up the canner) there is a savings of $1.15 for every 1 1/2 cups of beans that you pressure can yourself. Doing one batch of beans can save over $20.00.

You can make your own refried beans using home-canned beans. Drain any liquid (mine don't usually have extra liquid, but yours might) and then mash the beans up using a mixer, blender, or potato masher/pastry cutter. Then add some animal fat (bacon grease or lard is always good) and spices to taste. Here is a basic recipe:

> 1 quart canned beans
> 2 TB animal fat (melted) or oil
> 1-3 tsp. each of garlic powder, cumin, and chili powder
> Salt to taste

Mix everything together and add more spices if necessary. Heat up in the microwave or in a small sauce pan if you want the beans to be served warm.

Pasta: Again, I tend to buy pasta at discount stores or I wait for sales. Dollar Tree ('everything's a dollar') stores are a good place to stock up on pasta; recently I discovered spaghetti noodles there for $0.66 per pound. If you are checking pasta prices, make sure to notice the size of the box. A box does not always equal one pound. Some boxes are 12 oz., in which the final price per pound would be 25% more than the price of the box. At the Dollar Tree, boxes were 24 oz. each.

Sometimes Ibotta will offer a $0.25 rebate for any brand of pasta. If I purchase the very cheapest brand ($1.00/lb.) and use the rebate, it brings the price down to $0.75 per pound; comparable to prices I have found at the bent 'n' dent store. If I weren't shopping at Walmart, I would use the rebate at the Dollar Tree and get pasta for $0.50 per pound.

Keep in mind when planning meals that regularly-priced pasta is rarely the most nutritious OR cheapest carbohydrate to feed your family. If you are trying to eat for $10.00 per person, I would only make one or two pasta dishes per week and use rice, beans, potatoes or bread for the other meals.

<u>DIY Pasta</u>: I have made egg noodles before, but it takes a lot of time and doesn't save much money if you have to buy the eggs. Even if you have access to completely free eggs (unlikely, because you still have to buy feed for the chickens), the flour is still not free. Most of the time it is cheaper and easier to just buy store pasta at $0.75 (or less) per pound.

Specialty Grains: I tend to stay away from specialty grains like couscous or quinoa. They are much higher priced than your typical rice and beans. However, sometimes I can find these at the discount store for the same price as pasta. If I'm feeling adventurous, I'll buy it.

Foraging Grains

Many wild plants can be made into various flours, breakfast porridges, etc. Below are some ideas. It takes considerable time to harvest wild grains and make them into flour, and you only save about $0.11 per cup. I have only done it a few times, but I think it is still worth mentioning. The scope of this book is not large enough to cover cooking instructions, but I trust that you can find those elsewhere.

Acorns (*Quercus*): These can be roasted, hulled, and

ground into meal. You can use the meal half and half with regular flour to make bread, muffins or pancakes.

Beechnuts (*Fagus*): Can be roasted and ground for a coffee substitute. The inner bark can also be dried and pulverized to be used as bread flour.

Birch (*Betula*): The inner bark can be dried and ground into flour. It can also be cut into strips and boiled like noodles in stew.

Black Walnut (*Juglans*): Nuts can be extracted and used in baking and cooking.

Cattail (*Typha*): The golden pollen can be shaken off the flower spikes, collected, and used as a substitute for bread flour. The cores of the cattail, also, can be dried and ground into flour. Sift to remove any fibers.

Chickory (*Chichorium*): Roots of this plant can be slowly roasted in a partly open oven, until they have a crisp snap when broken. It can then be ground and used as a coffee substitute.
Clover (*Trifolium*): Seed-filled heads can be dried and ground into flour.

Dandelion (*Taraxacum*): Roots can be prepared in the same way as chickory, then used as a coffee stretcher or substitute.

Dock (*Rumex*): Seeds can be used to make flour. Rub the thin papery wings off of the seeds, and then sift for fineness before grinding into flour.

Green Amaranth (*Amaranthus*): When I was growing up, we called this plant "pigweed" or "red root". The seeds can be prepared in the same way as dock, and ground to make a nutritious flour.

Hazelnuts (*Corylus*): Use in cookies, candies and baked goods.

Hickory nuts (*Carya*): Use in baking, similar to black walnut or hazelnut.

Kentucky Coffee Tree (*Gymnocladus*): Beans can be roasted in the oven and ground into a coffee substitute. I am not a coffee drinker, but this substitute has a light enough flavor to appeal to me.

Lambsquarter (*Chenopodium*): The seeds can be ground into a dark meal, and mixed half and half with regular flour to be used in baking.

Maple seeds (*Acer*): Seeds of the maple tree can be hulled by pulling the "wings" off, and then roasted or boiled before being eaten.

Wild mustard (*Brassica*): The seeds of this plant can be used for homemade mustard by grinding the seeds and then adding enough vinegar to make a paste.

Pine (*Pinus*): The inner bark can be either dried and ground to be used half-and-half with flour, or it can be cut into strips and dried, being later boiled and eaten like noodles. The pine nuts, or pinions, can also be eaten as a snack or used in cooking after they have been roasted.

Poplar (*Populus*): Like pine and other trees, the inner bark of the poplar can be dried and ground into a flour additive/substitute, or it can be dried in strips and then cooked as noodles.

Purslane (*Portulaca*): The seeds of this plant can be ground and used half and half with regular flour.

Shepherd's Purse (*Capsella*): Seeds can be ground into meal.

Yellow Water Lily (*Nuphar*): The seed vessels can be fried and shelled, then cooked, buttered and salted like popcorn. They swell like popcorn, but do not crack. They can also be had with milk or cream as a breakfast cereal.

Breads

Almost all breads can be made at home. Sandwich bread, pita bread, French bread, tortillas, bagels, muffins- the whole nine yards. A general rule for buying bread is that the simpler breads can be bought almost as cheap as making them (especially when on sale), but more extravagant breads are worth making yourself.

Simple sandwich bread, for example, can be found at Walmart for $0.88 per loaf (if you buy the cheapest off-brand). If I use a $0.25 Ibotta rebate on the bread, it only costs $0.63. My homemade bread costs $0.58 for about two loaves, but that is not including the electricity/propane for heating up the oven. There is also more waste with homemade bread because it crumbles easier and only lasts a few days before starting to mold. At our house, I don't usually make bread at home. Instead, I plan meals that don't include bread. When I do find a steeply discounted loaf (for example, in the "day old" bin or a manager's special clearance), I buy it and celebrate by serving sandwiches. Or I will keep the bread in the pantry until an especially busy day when I don't have time to make a regular meal. Sandwiches utilizing discount bread are also fantastic food for road trips.

If I can get a one pound (average size) loaf of bread for $0.88, it costs twice as much as rice or potatoes. Eliminating bread from the meal plan will not only save money, but will eliminate a lot of empty calories (because let's admit it- bargain bread isn't the most nutritious thing around). Cutting out bread entirely is also an inexpensive way to be gluten free. Instead of making gluten-free breads, just start eating more rice and potato meals. Oats are another grain that can be used in replacement of wheat. I have found that oatmeal (or flour made from oatmeal) makes excellent gluten-free cookies, and it is much cheaper than almond or coconut flour to make yourself.

I've included my favorite bread recipe in *Pizza Night; A Simple Meal Plan*. It is a dual-purpose, no-frills refrigerator dough that can be used for bread, bagels, pizza crust, rolls and more.

Baking

A good way to save money on baking supplies is to simply stop baking. I only bake for potlucks, farmers market, and special occasions like birthdays or Christmas. This cuts down on use of expensive ingredients like chocolate chips, butter and/or nuts.

My two rules of thumb for baking supplies are 1) buy in bulk, and 2) buy at the discount store.

The Amish discount store an hour from our house usually has a good stock of baking supplies. We try to make a trip (or stop by on our way to another destination) three or four times per year. Many times these supplies are 50% off or more. Sometimes the store sells expired goods, so if you are shopping at a discount store and that concerns you, check before you buy. It does not bother me. If something is past its "best by" or "better by" date, it only means that the item is past <u>peak</u> freshness. It is by no means unsafe to use, and most likely no one you cook for is going to be able to tell the difference. "Use by" dates are what you need to watch out for, and these are mostly found on produce, milk, and meat products. I have noticed that the bent 'n' dent stores will freeze meat before it expires, and then put it out for sale in their freezers. If you have a problem with this, then don't buy the meat. Personally, I grew up eating frozen meat so it doesn't bother me.

Flour: I buy 25 lb. bags of white flour at Walmart. I do not do a lot of baking, so the quality of the flour does not matter to me, and the white flour is better to use for farmers market baked goods. I have also made oat flour from rolled oats in our Vitamix blender. You can only do this if you have a special "dry" container, though, or you could try using a food processer.

Sugar: Once again, I purchase white sugar in 25 lb. bags from Walmart. It is possible to make your own powdered or brown sugar in a pinch, but most of the time it is cheaper to just buy it.

Baking Chocolate: Re-melt or chop Christmas or Valentine's Day candy (bought on sale after the holidays) to use in baking. You can also find chocolate at discount stores.

Nuts: Buying nuts on a regular basis can get expensive. I only pay full price for nuts around Christmas, and if I do, I purchase them in bulk. Otherwise I will stock up on nuts at the bent 'n' dent stores in our area. I am not picky about whether the nuts are sliced, chopped, whole or pieces. All I care about is the price per pound. On a recent trip, I was able to find a package of almonds for $2.50 per pound, and cashews for $3.50 per pound. In our area, even bulk nuts hardly ever drop below $9.00 per pound at the grocery store.

You can also find nuts for free by foraging in the wild. Two nuts that grow on our property are hickory nuts and black walnuts. The hickory nuts take too much time to crack for such a small yield, but the black walnuts are worth doing if you have some extra time.

How to collect black walnuts:
1. Gather up a pail of the green walnuts and dump them on the driveway.
2. Run over the walnuts with your car several times.
3. Finish peeling the husk off the walnuts and leave the black inner nuts in a safe spot to dry for several months. The husk, while still green, can be made into black walnut tincture and is sometimes used to fight internal parasites.
4. When the nuts have dried, find a cement block/area and a hammer. Crack open the nuts and collect the meats in a plastic airtight container.

To save the most money on nuts, just don't use them. If a recipe calls for nuts and you don't have any discount nuts in your pantry, try using sunflower seeds. They have the same crunchy and salty factor without the price.

Yeast: Yeast should always be bought in bulk, not those little packets. Pour some of the bulk yeast into a small jar to refrigerate and use, and the rest can be kept fresh in the freezer until the jar is ready to be refilled. Some fermented recipes call for the use of wild yeast, which is free.

Baking Mixes: As I mentioned in the section on price lists, it is often cheaper to make cookies or brownies from a mix than from scratch. Keep track of how much every from-scratch recipe costs to make. I know that chocolate chip cookies cost $4.45 for me to make, so if I find a chocolate chip cookie mix that includes the chocolate chips for $0.75, you can bet I'll buy it. Even when you count the cost of the 1/3 cup butter and egg required to make the mix, you still come out way ahead.

Typically I will only find these kind of baking mix deals at the Amish discount store, and yes, they are usually expired (if only by a few months). I don't spend a lot of money on dessert mixes, though. They are only bought for "emergency" potluck meals, so one box per month is plenty.

When I was younger, I would try to make special foods for potlucks- guacamole, pesto, cheesecake, etc.- and it would often cost at least $5.00 every time. Now that I'm married and not trying to impress anyone, I frequently spend less than $1.00 per potluck by just bringing a cheap dessert. In our culture, few people care whether or not you made something from scratch, and some of the "best cooks" I know make everything from a mix. That's why it tastes so good. Why are we trying so hard to impress people with our from-scratch cooking, when the lady next door can bring Gordon's meatballs and everyone loves them?

Herbs & Spices

I love using herbs and spices. They provide more flavor for less expense than common ingredients like cheese, butter or sugar.

Free Flavor: Growing Your Own

It is very easy to grow many herbs and some spices at home. In my own garden, I have grown sage, basil, rosemary, thyme, dill, cilantro, coriander, garlic, mints, and mustard seeds. The mustard seeds were by far the most time consuming, but it did save money and was a fun project.

If you are growing a large quantity of any one herb, it is better to start it from seed. If you only want one plant though (sage or mint, for example, will grow back bigger every year), it is probably better to just buy the plant. This is especially true for herbs that are hard to start from seed, like rosemary or tarragon. In my area, herbs commonly sell for $3.00-$4.00 per plant. If you take into consideration that seed packets cost $2.00-$3.00, it might not be worth starting an herb from seed if only one plant survives to maturity. For example, I tried starting lavender from seed this year. A few of the seeds germinated, but only one plant survived to maturity. With all of the other seedlings I had to take care of, it was a hassle to baby my little lavender plant. I ended up buying a second plant, already grown, for just a little more than the lavender seed packet had cost me. For easy-germinating herbs like thyme or oregano, though, you may as well start from seed and reap more harvest for less money.

Spices, though just as easy to grow, are a little more time-consuming to harvest. Spices are usually the seed pods of a plant that have been ground into powder (or come in a grinder, so you can grind them right before using). Keep track of how much time you spend harvesting, and then determine whether the time you spent is worth the savings. If you saved $10.00 for an hour of harvesting, it's probably worth it. If you only saved $2.00, perhaps you are better off just buying the spice.

Other garden plants that provide flavor are garlic and chili peppers. Both are easy to grow. They can be used fresh, or dried and ground into powder.

More Free Flavor: Foraging

You don't HAVE to grow your own spices. Many spices grow on their own, in your own backyard. They are just waiting to be found! Some spices that come to mind are sumac, shepherd's purse, bayberry, or many of the sap-producing trees (for making syrup with). The possibilities of flavoring food with free, wild edibles are really limitless. An excellent book on this topic is *The New Wildcrafted Cuisine* by Pascal Baudar. Mr. Boudar uses everything from leaves and roots to rocks, dirt and insects in his cooking. I am not that hardcore, but it proves that flavor can come from almost anywhere, and a lot of it is free for the taking.

Bayberry (*Myrica*)- Leaves used for flavoring soups,

broths, stews, etc. since Colonial times.

Birch (*Betula*)- Sap can be boiled down to produce syrup.

Black Walnut (*Juglans*)- Sap can be boiled down to produce syrup. Nuts are also used for their distinct flavoring.

Butternut (*Juglans*)- Sap can be boiled down to produce syrup. Immature nuts can be used to make pickles. Nutmeats can also be used in salads, cookies, pies, etc.

Chickory (*Chichorium*)- Root used as a flavoring/substitute for coffee.

Clover (*Trifolium*)- Can be used for flavoring cheese (or eaten raw).

Chickweed (*Stellaria*) (*Alisine*)- Can be dried and used to replace dried parsley in recipes. You can also do this with any wild edible green.

Elderberry (*Sambucus*)- Flower blossoms of this plant can add flavor to pancakes, muffins and fritters.

Fireweed (*Epilobium*) (*Chamaenerion*)- Leaves can be dried and used to flavor tea, or make a satisfactory tea all by themselves.

Wild Grape (*Vitis*)- Leaves can be picked in the spring when they are still tender, and stored in a saturated salt solution until ready to made into stuffed grape leaves.

Wild Horseradish (*Armoracia*)- Root can be grated and mixed with sour cream to bring out the flavor in meat. Grated root can also be mixed with lemon juice and a pinch of sugar, made into a sauce and stored in the refrigerator until ready to be used.

Juniper (*Juniperus*)- Berries were traditionally used by Native Americans for baking, roasted as a coffee substitute, or crushed, sieved, and used like butter. Juniper tea can be made by boiling 12 small berry-less sprigs in a quart of water, and simmering for ten minutes. For very high Vitamin C content, steep overnight after you have simmered the brew.

Maple (*Acer*)- Maple trees can be tapped in the early spring, and sap collected for maple syrup. To make the syrup, you must boil down the watery sap until it is thick. Usually homemade syrup will be a little runnier than commercial maple syrup, but still good. One time when I was making maple syrup, I put a sachet of pumpkin pie spice in the boiling sap. The syrup was excellent.

Wild Mints (*Mentha*)- All sorts of mints can be used for flavoring teas, brews or meat dishes. Some are: Spearmint, Beebalm, Horsemint, Peppermint, Pennyroyal, or even Ground Ivy, which was traditionally used for flavoring beer. An easy way to identify plants in the mint family is to feel their stem. Is it round or square? Members of the mint family always have square stems. Even basil is in the mint family.

Wild Mustard (*Brassica*)- Seeds can be ground up, and enough vinegar added to make a paste. This can be used just like regular mustard. The whole seeds can also be used to flavor pickles, soups, barbeque sauce, and stews.

New Jersey Tea (*Ceanothus*)- Used by American Colonists during the Revolution, the leaves of this plant can be dried and used as any other herbal tea.

Pine (*Pinus*)- Needles can be used to make a tea high in Vitamin C. For even more Vitamin C, let the needles steep (after they've been covered in boiling water) overnight.

Plantain (*Plantago*)- use leaves to make tea; cover ½ handful in boiling water and steep for 30 minutes.

Prickly Pear (*Opuntia*)- Fruit can be made into candy, jelly, or pickles.

Wild Raspberry & Blackberry (*Rubus*)- Leaves can be used as an herbal tea.

Wild Rose (*Rosa*)- Petals, leaves and roots can be used to make tea. Use one teaspoon dried material (twice that for fresh) and cover with one cup boiling water. Steep for five minutes. A little bit of sweetener will bring out the flavor.

Salsify (*Tragopogon*)- Roots can be roasted and ground to make a coffee substitute.

Serviceberry (*Amelanchier*)- Historically used by Native Americans to flavor pemmican.

Spicebush (*Benzoin*)- Leaves, twigs, and bark can be simmered in one quart of water for 15 minutes in order to make tea. Dried and powdered, these parts can be used as a substitute for allspice.

Wild Strawberry (*Fragaria*)- Leaves can be made into tea. For medicinal-quality Vitamin C, immerse fresh-picked, green, young strawberry leaves with boiling water, cover and drink cold the next day.

Sumac (*Rhus*)- Berries were traditionally used by Native Americans and Colonists to make a sort of "lemonade". The berries can also be dried, powdered and used as a citrus-y spice.

Toothwort (*Dentaria*)- Grate the roots, mix with vinegar, and serve as a condiment for salads or sandwiches.

Wild Ginger (*Asarum*)- Root can be used like store-bought ginger.

Buying Herbs & Spices

If I am looking for a spice, I start at Walmart. Many of their spices only cost $1.00 for a 2 oz. container. In some cases, that container will last me for years. A few of the more popular spices (onion powder, garlic powder, chili powder) are actually available in 1 lb. containers at Walmart.

If the spice is more expensive at Walmart (cloves and ginger, for example, are $4.00-$5.00 for a 1 oz. container), I will try to buy it in bulk at a health food or specialty store. Some of these bulk spices are over 50% cheaper than if you buy them in a little container. Spices I've bought in bulk include ginger, cloves, cream of tartar and cardamom.

Lastly, you can find cheap spices, hit or miss, at discount stores. Recently I purchased just over ½ oz. of "Herbs de Provence" at a discount store for $1.25. I was not familiar with the spice and honestly couldn't tell if I was getting a deal or not. However, it was almost as cheap as the Walmart spices and it came in a lovely glass container that I'll be able to reuse for my own home-grown spices.

Last year, at the same discount store, I found two jars of mulling spice mix for $1.50 each. I used one of the jars for cider. With the other jar, I spent an hour or so separating out the individual spices: whole cloves, whole nutmeg, whole allspice, lemon and orange peels, and cinnamon bark. For $1.50, I was able to get six different spices in small quantities that I would actually be able to use. Had I bought the spices separately, I would have spent a lot more money.

Spice Mixes: Sometimes when I am shopping at the

discount store, I will buy pre-mixed seasoning packets. In the past these have included things like "Italian herb baked chicken & pasta", "chicken tinga seasoning mix", "zesty sour cream seasoning mix", "baja citrus marinade" or "beef bourguignon family seasoning mix". I use these when I think my cooking needs a little help.

Below are some homemade spice mixes that you can make yourself.

Seasoned Salt

8 TB salt
3 TB pepper
2 TB paprika
½ TB onion powder
½ TB garlic powder
Mix and store in airtight container.

Poultry Seasoning

1 TB rosemary
1 TB oregano
1 TB thyme
2 tsp. sage
2 tsp. ginger
1 tsp. black pepper

Mix all ingredients together and store in airtight container.

Chili Powder

 1/4 c. paprika
 1 TB garlic powder
 1 TB cayenne pepper
 1 TB onion powder
 1 TB oregano
 2 TB cumin

 Mix all ingredients together and store in an airtight container.

Ranch Dressing Mix

 10 saltines, crushed
 3/4 c. parsley flakes
 1/4 c. dried minced onion
 1/4 c. onion powder
 1/4 c. garlic powder
 1 TB dried dill weed
 Mix together and store in airtight container.

Enchilada Sauce Mix

 2 TB mild chili powder
 2 TB. paprika
 2 TB. cornstarch
 4 1/2 tsp. salt
 4 1/2 tsp. dried onions flakes
 1 TB sugar
 1 TB ground cumin
 1 TB garlic powder

1 1/2 tsp. oregano
1 1/2 tsp. ground coriander
3/4 tsp. cayenne pepper

Mix all ingredients together and store in an airtight container. To use, mix 6 oz. tomato paste with 2 cups of water (or 1 pint canned tomato sauce/puree). Add spice mix to taste.

Spaghetti Sauce Mix

Here is a spice mix you can add to tomato sauce (or tomato paste and water) to make a delicious spaghetti sauce.

1/4 c. cornstarch
1/4 c. dried minced onion
3 TB dried celery flakes
1/4 cup dried parsley flakes
2 TB Italian seasoning
4 tsp. salt
4 tsp. sugar
2 tsp. dried minced garlic

Use ¼ cup of the spice mix with 6 oz. tomato paste and 2 cups water. You can also use ¼ cup of spice mix with one pint of homemade tomato sauce.

Taco Seasoning

2 TB chili powder
4 ½ tsp. cumin
5 tsp. paprika

1 TB onion powder

2 ½ tsp. garlic powder

¼ tsp. cayenne pepper

Mix and store in airtight container.

Fats & Oils

It used to be that low-fat and no-fat diets were "healthiest". Now conventional wisdom has swung to the opposite side, and some folks have gone to the other extreme; advocating a high fat diet with only the purest, finest, most expensive fats: raw grass-fed organic butter, extra virgin olive oil, expeller pressed coconut oil. While there is certainly nothing wrong with these fats, they probably won't fit into a $10.00 per week food budget. A high fat diet is a high cost diet.

To have the perfect amount of fat in your diet, I think it is enough to eat foods that naturally include fat; things like milk, eggs, or meat. We don't need to ADD fat to our diets; let's just refrain from buying unnatural, artificially low-fat or no-fat foods.

Here are some fats that we eat and cook with on a regular basis.

Bacon grease: when cooking bacon, I save the grease and use it to fry eggs with. Sometimes I will use a dab of grease in soups to add flavor as well.

Butter: I don't do much baking, so this cuts down on butter use a lot. I might go through one pound per month between the two of us and any cookies I bake. We also use butter to fry eggs if there is no bacon grease (not a common occurrence). I have found that the cheapest way to buy butter is 1) when it goes on sale, 2) in 2-lb. packs at Walmart, 3) in single one pound lumps as opposed to sticks, or 4) at the restaurant supply store. The price of butter (like milk) goes up and down, so your price book is essential here. Butter freezes well, so whenever I find a low price, I stock up.

In the last year, I have started making butter with cream from my goat's milk. After the milk has set for a few days in the fridge, a thin layer of cream will rise to the top. I have a freezer box specifically for cream, and every week or so I skim the tops of my jars and add the cream to my cream collection in the freezer. When the box is full, I thaw it and pour it into my blender, blending it on medium speed. In 20-30 seconds, the cream starts to splash around, which means the butter has separated from the buttermilk.

I rinse the buttermilk out of the butter using cold, cold water. I keep changing the water and kneading the butter until the water comes out clear. Then I put the lump of butter in the fridge.

Goat butter does go rancid faster and has a softer texture than regular butter. If I'm not using it right away, I put the butter in the freezer. I'm able to collect 8-16 ounces of butter every month this way, for free.

Olive oil: I use olive oil to fry vegetables or make salad dressings with. We buy the one-gallon jugs of regular olive oil. If you are buying the cheapest brand, just make sure that it is 100% olive oil, and not olive oil mixed with soybean or something like that.

Canola oil: this is a cheaper, not-as-healthy oil that I use primarily for making granola or other baking. Like olive oil, I buy this in one-gallon jugs.

Lard or other animal fats: I use lard sometimes for making pie crusts, though I believe butter works and tastes better. We also have used rendered animal fats to fry vegetables or eggs with, but personally I think the flavor is a bit strong.

How to use extra fats: I do a lot of meat canning, and oftentimes a layer of fat will form at the top. Chicken fat is too soft to pick off easily, but if the fat is hardened (as in the case of beef, venison, lamb, etc.) I will use a fork to pull it out of the jar and put it in my "fat box" in the freezer. When the box is full, I re-melt all of the fat scraps together and strain out any meat pieces. This new fat mixture can be used for making soap (or cooking, if you don't mind the flavor). I also find fat scraps on cooked roasts that have been refrigerated, or in the bottom of my pressure canner after canning meat. **Note:** the pressure canner fat pieces are only used for soap, not human consumption.

Sauces & Condiments

Tomato Based Sauces: Any sauce that is tomato-based-spaghetti sauce, pizza sauce, marinara, or enchilada sauce- can be made using tomato paste (I also use tomato paste to make chili with, instead of buying tomato juice). Just add water until you get the right consistency, and then add the proper spices and/or additional ingredients.

Many tomato based sauces at the grocery store cost at least $1.00 per jar. Tomato paste is often a more economical (but not too labor-intensive) way to make your own sauces. If you buy a larger can and cannot use it all right away, extra paste can be frozen in ice cube trays or also frozen sausage-link style in individual meal portions.

The cheapest way to acquire tomato-based sauces is by growing all or most of the ingredients- certainly the tomatoes- in your own garden. Even if you factor in the cost of new canning lids, home grown tomato sauces are pennies on the dollar compared to store bought, and probably healthier, too.

White Sauce: A white sauce (or "roux") is just a mixture of fat, flour and liquid. Most of my white sauces contain meat, so this is how I make them.

1. Brown meat.
2. Toss a handful of white flour in the browned meat (burner still turned on) and stir thoroughly.

154

3. When the meat/flour mixture starts to thicken, add milk until it is as thin as you want it.

4. Continue adding either flour or milk until you have reached the desired amount and/or consistency.

Pesto: There are three things you can do to make pesto more affordable: 1) grow your own basil or used foraged plant matter (wild mustard, etc.), 2) use sunflower seeds instead of nuts, and 3) use any inexpensive sharp-flavored cheese you can find, not necessarily parmesan. The pesto will be a little different, but still great. A "medicinal/antibacterial" pesto can be made by increasing the amount of garlic. Here is my recipe:

½ cup sunflower seeds
3 TB chopped garlic
5 cups packed basil (or other green herbs)
1 tsp. black pepper
1 ½ cup olive oil
1 cup shredded or ½" cubed cheese

Blend/process sunflower seeds and garlic first. Then add leaves, then pepper and olive oil, and lastly add the cheese. Freeze in ice cube trays (covered with plastic wrap) and then store cubes in a freezer bag. For maximum flavor, try to minimize exposure to air. My pesto always turns brown wherever it has been exposed to air.

Bean Dip: Use garbanzo beans to make hummus.

Peanut Butter: If you do happen to find extremely cheap (perhaps stale) peanuts, you can make them into peanut butter using a food processor or blender. Peanut butter can also be found on sale once or twice a year. It has a long shelf life, so when you find a great deal, stock up! But keep in mind that 1) any kind of nut butter is rather expensive when you compare it to other sandwich spreads, 2) there are no cheap homemade recipes for the condiment, and 3) most of us cannot grow peanuts in the garden. For this reason I use peanut butter quite sparingly; a couple times per year I make cookies with it, but that's about all I use it for.

Jams & Jellies: You can make your own jam or jelly with free foraged fruit. The only other ingredients you will need are pectin and sugar. I purchase pectin on sale. Last year I found some no-sugar-required pectin (steeply discounted) that I have been using with a small amount of honey in each jar. There are also some jams you can make without pectin, depending on the type of fruit. Apples, for example, contain a lot of their own pectin.

If you are working with pitted or seedy fruit, jelly is easier to make than jam because you only use the juice. For example, wild black cherries or wild grapes could be easily made into jelly, but would require a lot more work to make jam because there is a lot more pit than actual fruit.

Honey: Typically honey is not very cheap, but it is cheaper to buy in bulk. I have heard that processers are allowed to add a certain amount of corn syrup to honey before they sell, so be careful where you buy. To rejuvenate crystallized honey, simply place the open jar in an oven at 250 degrees Fahrenheit and heat until the honey liquefies. If your honey is in a plastic container, you can do the same thing by placing it in a bowl of very hot tap water.

Pickles: You can make pickles at home with garden produce. It is also possible to make pickles with foraged ingredients like cattail shoots, glasswort or prickly pear.

Turn pickle juice into salad dressing by mixing it with oil, or use it to marinate thinly sliced cucumbers or beets. You can also make pickled hard boiled eggs by marinating boiled eggs in the leftover pickle juice. Refrigerated, the eggs will keep for a month.

Salad Dressings: Below are some recipes for salad dressing that you can make at home. As always, make sure a recipe is actually cheaper to make than it is to buy. Sometimes it is cheaper to buy a $0.75 bottle of discount salad dressing than make one.

Thousand Island Dressing
¾ cup mayonnaise
1 TB sweet pickle relish
2 TB ketchup
2 TB finely chopped green bell pepper
2 TB finely chopped onion

1 TB lemon juice

½ tsp. sugar

¼ tsp. Worcestershire sauce

1 hard-cooked egg, chopped

Combine all ingredients in a small bowl except egg. Stir in chopped egg last. Refrigerate. Makes 1 1/3 cup.

Ranch Salad Dressing

1 cup mayonnaise

1 cup buttermilk

1 TB finely chopped green onion tops

¼ tsp onion powder

2 tsp minced parsley

¼ tsp garlic powder or 1 garlic clove, finely minced

¼ tsp. paprika

1/8 tsp cayenne pepper

¼ tsp salt

¼ tsp black pepper

Combine all ingredients in a small bowl. Refrigerate. Makes 2 cups.

Honey BBQ Sauce

1.5 c. Ketchup

1/2 c. Brown sugar

1/2 c. White vinegar

1/2 c. Honey

2 TB soy sauce

1 TB vegetable oil

1 TB minced onion

1 tsp. Ginger

1 tsp. Salt

1 tsp. Dry mustard

1 tsp. Garlic powder

1 tsp. Black pepper

Simmer all ingredients over medium heat for 10 minutes. Store in airtight container in the refrigerator for 2 months.

Copycat Catalina Dressing

2/3 cup ketchup

½ cup sugar

2/3 cup vegetable oil

½ cup red wine vinegar

Salt to taste

1-2 gloves garlic

1 TB finely minced onion

Combine all ingredients in a jar with a tight-fitting led and shake. This can also be mixed in a blender, although the color is slightly changed. If preparing in a blender, stir in onion last, by hand. Refrigerate. Makes 2 cups.

Cucumber Buttermilk Dressing

1 cup buttermilk

¼ cup grated cucumber

2 TB minced green onions, white and green parts

1 TB Dijon-style mustard

2 tsp minced fresh parsley

2 tsp lemon juice

¼ tsp dried dill

¼ tsp freshly ground black pepper

Combine all ingredients in a small bowl with a tight lid. Stir or shake well. Refrigerate. Makes 1 ¼ cups.

Italian Vinaigrette

½ cup red wine vinegar

1 ½ cups olive oil

2 cloves garlic, crushed

¾ tsp salt

¾ tsp black pepper

1 TB dry mustard

½ tsp. dried basil or oregano

Combine ingredients in a large jar with a tight-fitting lid. Shake well. Makes 1 quart.

Blue Cheese Dressing

This recipe makes a large quantity and is very strong.

1 qt. mayonnaise

1 cup buttermilk

1 cup small-curd cottage cheese

1 tsp Worcestershire sauce

1 tsp garlic salt

1 tsp salt

4 oz. Roquefort or blue cheese, crumbled

Combine all ingredients in a medium bowl except crumbled cheese. Mix well with electric mixer. Stir in crumbled cheese with a fork. Refrigerate. Makes 1 ½ quarts.

Desserts

Desserts can be very easy to do on a limited budget. One option is to use discount dessert mixes (these will cost about $0.75, plus $0.25 for the oil and egg). Jello is also inexpensive to use, and one of my favorite ways to make desserts is with free fruit. Using fruit as a base is a lot cheaper than using chocolate, peanut butter, cream cheese, or even whipped topping as a base. Fruit cobblers, crisps, pies and tarts are especially frugal. A little bit of butter, sugar and flour is all that is required in the way of baking supplies, and the rest is fruit, spices, and/or cornstarch.

The savings from baking your own pies are enormous IF you can find free fruit. I can make a fruit crisp for $1.47, a tart for $1.41, pie for $1.10, and cobbler for $0.93. Pies often sell for $6.00-$10.00 at the grocery store, and even more at a bakery, farmers market or specialty shop. If you are not a "boxed cake mix" kind of person and want to make dessert on a dime, fruit-based pastries are the way to go.

Fruit can also be used as a base for "ice cream". I use a handful of frozen fruit, along with some homemade yogurt and sweetener, and blend it up to make a super-thick smoothie that you have to eat with a spoon. If you don't have a powerful blender, you can try this with a food processor. Because the fruit is free, one serving of this ice cream costs less than $0.25. It is also a lot healthier than store bought ice cream.

Lastly, fruit can be used as a sweetener. Bananas,

cherries, pomegranates, mangos, figs and grapes have a high sugar content. If you use these fruits, you won't have to add as much sweetener (which, unlike the fruit, is NOT usually free). I really like using ripe bananas to sweeten smoothies, and have also used them to sweeten pudding, pancakes and other baked goods. Applesauce, if you make it with free apples, can be used to replace oil (and probably some of the sugar, as well) in baked goods.

Birthday Cake

Making your own birthday cakes will save a LOT of money. You can make a cake from scratch if you want, OR you can buy a cake mix and frosting at the discount store.

It is not super hard to learn basic cake decorating skills. You'll need some piping tips, bags (or you can make your own from plastic storage bags) and something to rotate the cake with if you chose to do round cakes. When I was first learning, I used an old carousel spice rack to do the job. A special round-edged spreading tool is helpful, but you can also use a knife.

The most important skills are spreading the frosting without breaking off pieces of the cake, and also making borders with the piping bag. I've taken some basic Wilton cake decorating classes, but you can probably learn it on your own. Here are some tips:

1. Make sure to use plenty of icing. The icing will STICK to

the cake, so if you lift your knife up and the icing sticks to the knife, it will bring up a ton of little cake crumbs with it. Then larger parts of the cake will start to break off, and you will have a mess of cake and icing. Instead, buy or make a lot more icing than you think you'll need. Use a spatula and put the WHOLE container on top of your cake. Remember, you cannot lift the icing off the cake. Spread the plop around, being sure to not let the knife get close to the cake itself. You can always take off extra when the cake is completely frosted, but trying to add more once you've started to spread it around can be challenging.

2. For borders, look at the grocery store bakery cakes for ideas. Some of the borders are just multi-colored squiggly lines over the edges. You can do this by filling 3-5 bags with different colored icing (white can be dyed with food coloring) and using a small round tip (size 3).

3. Lastly, there are plenty of pre-made cake decorations you can buy and use (sprinkles, edible letters and numbers, etc.) at discount stores, or you can use things in your home to decorate the cake with.

Snacks

Snacks are just that- snacks. They are not meals. Therefore, it is okay to ration snacks. Use bowls or bags and give a portion to each child (or person... including yourself!) and when it is gone, it is gone. This will not only save money, but save appetites for real meals like lunch and dinner. Healthy snack ideas include fresh fruits, carrots & ranch dip (made with Greek yogurt), homemade bread & jam, popsicles (chocolate pudding pops), popcorn, muffins, pita bread w/bean dip, smoothies, homemade crackers and cheese, or select types of cookies (lemon bars, not monster cookies!).

Chocolate Pudding Pops
　　　　1 1/2 cups sugar
　　　　3 TB cornstarch
　　　　1/2 tsp salt
　　　　1/2 cup cocoa powder OR 3 oz. unsweetened or bittersweet chocolate
　　　　3 cups milk
　　　　3 egg yolks, slightly beaten
　　　　1 1/2 tsp vanilla
　　　　1 TB butter
　　　　Combine sugar, cornstarch, salt, cocoa powder and milk in a saucepan. Cook over medium heat, stirring constantly, until mixture thickens and begins to boil. Boil one minute. Remove from heat. Slowly add pudding mixture to egg yolks. Return pudding to pan. Add vanilla and butter. Boil for one minute. Let mixture cool slightly. Fill popsicle molds and freeze until frozen

solid (about 3 hours).

Makes 8-9 popsicles.

Making Gelatin

Buy bulk unflavored gelatin instead of packets. It keeps indefinitely. You can make gelatin snacks or dessert the traditional way by dissolving 1 TB gelatin powder in 1 cup of hot liquid, adding 1 cup cold liquid and refrigerating until set. Whatever liquid you use, the gelatin will be more appealing if it has a nice color (green or brown are not appetizing!). To make "jigglers", double the amount of unflavored powdered gelatin.

A faster and more fool-proof method is to make gelatin in the blender. By using the blender as opposed to the "stir powder in hot water and add cold water" method, the gelatin will mix completely and not be "sandy" on the bottom.

Blender Gelatin
4 cups frozen fruit
2 TB unflavored gelatin powder
½ cup sugar
Hot water

Thaw one quart of frozen berries and puree it in the blender. Strain out the seeds (if desired) and pour back into the blender. Add unflavored gelatin and sugar. Add hot water to the 5-cup line and blend until smooth. Pour into pan and refrigerate until completely set.

Beverages

I talked a little bit about beverages in the section on buying health food. Basically, my husband and I drink mostly water, with a little bit of tea, kombucha or other homemade beverages here and there. We do not make a habit of buying soda, store bought smoothies/kefir/kombucha, alcoholic beverages or even milk to drink. During the summer my husband likes Gatorade (we buy the powder), and sometimes I will make homemade soda pop. If you have reusable glass bottles with caps and use free flavoring ingredients (foraged wild grapes, for example), the cost of each bottle is about $0.10. There is a bit of science involved with fermentation so I won't give recipes here, but there are plenty of books available on the topic.

During the winter we like to indulge in hot chocolate every now and then. Here is a good from-scratch recipe I use. Each cup costs about $0.20.

Hot Chocolate
2 tsp. sugar and a pinch of salt
1 tsp. cocoa
1 cup milk
Mix together the sugar, salt and cocoa and put into a small sauce pan. Add about 1 tsp. or so of the cold milk and stir well into a paste. Stirring a bit of the milk in first helps the cocoa to not clump. Add the rest of the milk then, and heat to just below boiling. Serve warm.

Feeding Dinner Guests

One of the most challenging aspects of the $10.00 per week plan will be having other families over for dinner. Instead of spending $0.65 per person for a meal, you will have to feed TWO people for that amount! You might go a little over budget during meals that include dinner guests, but strategic meal planning for the rest of the week (having corn meal mush for breakfast more often than eggs, or fixing more vegetarian meals) can make up for that one day of over spending. Soup is always a good dollar-stretcher when you are trying to feed a crowd.

One of my favorites is chili. Start with a can or two of tomato paste ($2.00) and thin with water until you've got the desired consistency. Then you can add beans ($0.35 per pint for home-canned beans), corn, sweet peppers or other vegetables from the garden, and meat. One pound of cheap meat ($2.00 for ground beef, less for sausage, turkey, venison, or other ground meat) can go a long way, or you can skip the meat altogether and just put more beans in. Lastly, spice the chili with cumin, chili powder, and salt to taste. Serve with sour cream ($1.30) for garnish. If you want to get really fancy, the soup can be served in bread bowls; hollowed out, homemade dinner rolls ($0.78). The bread bowls will be fancier, and they will also save money because you won't have to buy crackers. Keep the insides of the bowls to make crouton pieces out of. These can be used as garnish in replacement of cheese.

Using the method above, you can probably get away with

feeding 10 people for around $5.00-$7.00. The better you are at finding free food (namely meat and vegetables), the cheaper this meal will be. The nice thing about tomato paste chili is that you can just add more water if you think there won't be enough for everyone.

If dinner guests are going to be a common occurrence at your house, you need to start budgeting extra grocery money to allow for that. I think $1.00 per person, per meal would be appropriate. It's a little more than you would budget for a normal meal, but you will want the food to be a little nicer for guests. So if you're going to have five people over for dinner, give yourself an extra $5.00 that week for grocery money. If you're only budgeting $10.00 per person, per week but actually feeding MORE people than that, you will either run out of food, or money, or both.

Cooking With Leftovers

There are two problems that people run into when dealing with leftovers.

1. **People refuse to eat the leftovers**. This can be because the leftovers have been in the fridge for too long and have become unappealing (slimy, taste funny, etc.), or because family members had the same meal yesterday and are tired of it.

2. **Leftovers go bad in the fridge**. Apart from people refusing to eat leftovers, the biggest waste happens when you forget about them in the back of the fridge and they start growing mold. Or, perhaps you know they are there, but nobody feels like eating them before they start to deteriorate.

Freezing leftovers right away after you are done eating fixes both of these problems. It keeps the food just as fresh as the day they were made. A week later when everyone is hungry and you have NO dinner plan, it is easy to pull the leftovers out of the freezer and microwave them. Normally people don't mind eating the same meal they had a week earlier, and they may not even know the difference between a fresh meal and one that has been thawed and reheated.

I try to keep only a week's worth of leftovers in the freezer. That way it will not develop freezer burn, nor pile up so high that you have no room for more important freezer items.

Using Bits & Pieces: If there are not enough leftovers for an entire meal, you can use bits and pieces from different meals to make a whole new dish. Soup and casserole are popular revamped leftover meals. If you want to, you can keep all of the meat scraps in one container, veggie scraps in another, etc., until you have enough to make soup out of. You can also create a casserole by mixing meat, veggies, some type of carbohydrate (rice, potatoes, pasta, etc.) together with a binder (egg, white sauce, tomato sauce, etc.) and baking it at 350 degrees Fahrenheit for one hour, covered with tin foil. If all of the ingredients are pre-cooked, you can get away with cooking it for only 30 minutes, or until it is warmed through.

When you put leftovers in the freezer, it gives you "freezer meals" to have on hand without all the hassle and plastic bags needed for actual freezer meals. By eliminating leftover waste, you save money on groceries AND save cooking time. Some people intentionally cook twice as much food as they need and freeze the rest for another day. Because of the freezer space this requires, I chose to only freeze actual leftovers (mostly bits and pieces) to use in future meals, and prefer 2-for-1 meals (see Part 2) to freezer meals as a form of time/energy efficient cooking.

Restaurant Savings

I know that eating out is not usually a part of the frugal housewife's agenda. However, let's just say "it happens". Not only does it happen, but eating out can be a fun and meaningful part of life... without breaking the bank. Here are a few tips:

Basic Rules

1. **Only take two people.** Because we don't have any kids yet, my husband and I can get away with eating out every week and it doesn't cost too much. Families with children can do a weekly or biweekly child/parent "date", taking a different child along each time.

2. **Don't order drinks or dessert.** We order water most of the time, which is free, and if we feel hungry for dessert we will buy something at the grocery store or a McDonalds ice cream cone.

3. **Order a sandwich or lunch meal, not a dinner entree.** I have noticed that hamburgers cost between $8.00 and $11.00, but actual dinner meals cost $12.00 and up. To us, a burger that comes with fries is just as good as a plate of spaghetti with corn and coleslaw.

4. **Pick a cheaper restaurant.** One of the easiest ways to

save on eating out (besides foregoing it) is to find a cheaper restaurant to go to. Fine sit-down dining with local asparagus and microbrews will usually run about $13.00-$20.00 per person, per meal in our area. Chain or franchise sit-down restaurants often cost $8.00-$15.00 per meal. Nicer sandwich shops cost between $5.00-$10.00, and fast food is usually under $5.00 per person, for us.

A Plan for Cheaper Date Nights

If you are set on having a weekly date night, try this:

Week 1: Free date. Pack a picnic lunch and attend a free community event (or take a walk, go bird-watching, or do some other free activity).

Week 2: Sandwich/coffee shop date. Have breakfast, snack or a light meal on this date.

Week 3: Sit-down restaurant. Pick a nice chain restaurant to go to. Don't forget your coupon/birthday freebie/ email incentive!

Week 4: Fine dining! Once a month, pick a very nice restaurant to go to. This can be for a birthday, anniversary, celebration or other special event. You can bring coupons or use gift cards if you have them.

Changing up your date night by spending $0.00, $10.00,

$20.00, and $30.00 (a total of $50.00/month) is cheaper than getting stuck in a rut and going to the same old chain restaurant and spending $20.00 every week (a total of $80.00/month). My estimated numbers may differ from where you live. Lastly, when budgeting for restaurants, don't forget to add tax (6% in Michigan where we are) and tip (5%-20%, depending on the restaurant). That means your $10.00 burger actually costs $12.00! All the more reason to find a coupon.

Coupons & Free Stuff

Go out for a birthday. Almost all restaurants will offer a birthday freebie (usually dessert). Some restaurants will give you a free meal coupon good during the month of your birthday (or birthday of a family member). At the time of this writing, restaurants with free meals include Denny's, Bob Evans (meal for kids only), IHOP, Johnny Rockets, Perkins (free breakfast), Red Robin and Ruby Tuesday. Keep in mind that many of the free birthday meals require the purchase of one adult entree.

Sign up for the e-club. Many restaurants will send you some type of coupon as an incentive when you sign up for their marketing emails. Coupons include free appetizers, drinks, or sometimes even a free meal.

Sign up for the rewards program. If you frequent a certain restaurant, it might be worth it to sign up for their rewards club, where you can get a free gift after you spend a certain amount there.

Buy gift cards. During certain times of the year (Christmas and graduation/Father's Day come to mind), restaurants will run gift card sales such as "buy $25.00 in cards and get $5.00 free". Determine whether you eat at the restaurant enough to warrant buying that many gift cards, and make sure the cards won't expire before you use them. Also consider buying gift cards on sale if you plan on taking another family out to dinner (and therefore will spend the required $25.00 or $50.00 at the restaurant in question).

Look for coupons. You can find these in the newspaper, in junk mail, or even on the back of store receipts. When you find a coupon for a local restaurant, read the fine print (make sure drink purchases aren't required- that wouldn't be frugal!) and write the expiration date and name of the restaurant on the back of the coupon envelope. I keep my envelope in my purse at all times. If we are out and about and feel like eating at a restaurant, I check the coupon envelope to make sure we're not missing out on any free stuff or discounts.

One sweltering July day, we were early for church music practice. Hubs and I decided to head across the parking lot for smoothies at a local coffee shop. All of a sudden, I remembered my coupon envelope! Sure enough, I had a buy-1-get-1-free coupon for that very location. We ended up getting two drinks for the price of one.

As with any coupon, you have to read the fine print and NOT feel obligated to eat out simply because you have a coupon. The coupons are only used when you have already decided to eat out; for example, on a weekly date night or yearly birthday lunch.

Get the app on your phone. Many fast food restaurants now have apps that you can download to your smart phone. Most of these apps are just for online ordering, but a few of them offer weekly coupons or incentives for downloading. At the time of this writing, Auntie Anne's pretzel shop offers a free pretzel when you download their app, and McDonalds has "Free Fries Friday", where they will send you an e-coupon for free medium fries with any purchase made on a Friday.

Dine at certain hours. Some restaurants offer discounts (50% off appetizers, for example) if you come in an hour or so before closing, and some have a "happy hour" where drinks or appetizers are half off in the late afternoon.

Try calling your local pizza place right before closing and ask if they've had any "flops" or no-shows. You might just get a discount! As a side note, you can also ask for free empty pickle jars to use for storing dry goods like pasta or cornmeal.

Free Food Challenge

Here are some things you can do to drastically lower your grocery bill by finding free food.

1. Butcher a chicken.

2. Find a weed in your backyard that you can use to make salad.

3. Forage for berries and put them in the freezer.

4. Try collecting black walnuts, hickory nuts, or other native nuts and harvesting the nutmeats.

5. Go dumpster diving, if you live in the city.

6. Barter with a farmer friend for free meat.

7. Go fishing. Learn how to clean, gut and cook the fish.

8. Using a $0.25 "any brand" Ibotta rebate, see if there are any produce items you can buy in small amounts and get for free.

9. Transplant a berry bush or strawberry plant.

10. Build a raised bed and grow some vegetables in it.

11. Grow your own mint or chamomile for herbal tea.

Part 2: Cooking

This section is dedicated to all of the Cooks out there. To those of you who can make something out of nothing- the seed-starting, wheat-grinding, bread-baking, cheese-making, pressure-canning, sausage-stuffing, genius DIYers. You help us make the most of our groceries.

Save Time & Money with Tools

The first step to a great cooking experience is acquiring the right tools. To make food prep and preservation easy, here are some time- and labor-saving devices you may want to invest in:

Pots and Pans: My set of pots and pans is stainless steel. I have four different size pots (ranging from 1 quart to 8 quarts) and three different skillets, also of varying sizes from 7 inch to 12 inches in diameter. The set came with four lids to fit all of the pots.

I use a small cast iron pan to cook scrambled eggs every morning. I choose to use this pan because cleanup is easy. If you wait until the pan is hot before adding oil, it will create a non-stick surface. After you are done, you can just wipe out the pan and put it back.

To season a cast iron pan, coat the inside of the pan with vegetable oil or shortening. Place in the oven at 250 degrees Fahrenheit for 30 minutes. Remove the pan from the oven, wipe off excess oil, and return it to the oven for another 30 minutes. Then turn the oven off and leave the pan in overnight. If your pan is new, this might need to be done again. During the seasoning process, oil is soaked up into the pan, which is what makes it "non-stick". NEVER wash a cast iron pan with hot or soapy water, as this will remove the oil. They also need to be thoroughly dry before putting away, otherwise they will rust.

Knives: Often-used cutlery includes a chef's knife for chopping, serrated knife for slicing bread, tomatoes, and citrus fruits, and a utility knife for miscellaneous slicing and chopping. As amateur butcherers, my husband and I also have two boning knives. The boning knives were surprisingly hard to find, but we did finally get some from Macy's department store. A swivel-bladed vegetable peeler and paring knife are also very helpful.

I have three cutting boards: one large wooden board for large things like watermelon and pineapple, and two small plastic boards for average sized produce and meat. The designated meat cutting board has a piece of brown string tied on it so I don't get the two mixed up. You don't want to accidentally cross-contaminate uncooked vegetables with raw meat juices.

Basic Cookware: Measuring cups, wooden spoons & spatula (if you use enamel or nonstick pots and pans), tongs, rubber spatula, long-handled cooking spoon, metal spatulas, long-handled slotted spoon, pancake turner, wire whisk, rolling pin, metal colander, funnels (one small & one large), wire rack, oven thermometer, meat thermometer, ladle, pot holders, and kitchen timer.

Other Useful Equipment: Salad spinner, pastry brush, cheesecloth, garlic mincer/press, and crock pot.

High-end equipment: The two expensive tools I have in

my kitchen are a Kitchen Aid stand mixer, and a Vitamix blender.

The Kitchen Aid is an essential time-saver for any kind of mixing task. In addition to mixing, you can also buy different attachments to do everything from noodle making to sausage stuffing.

The Vitamix actually does the work of a blender, food processer, knife & cutting board, and spice grinder. Right now I use the blender most for chopping onions and dicing potatoes and carrots. I've also used it to make fruit-based ice cream, goat's milk butter, soups, condiments like pesto and mayonnaise, smoothies, and beverages. Recently I used it to grate soap for homemade laundry detergent. The dry container (a separate purchase) functions as a grinder and allows me to powder herbs from my own garden, make flours, crush graham cracker crumbs and much more. The blender, as opposed to any other tool, is easy to clean and quick to use. Certain relatives think I sound like a salesman when I talk about the high-end blender that we have in our kitchen. However, I'm continually amazed at what it can do.

Food Preservation Equipment

There are a few more things you will want to have if you plan on establishing an extensive pantry and eating for $10.00 per week.

1. **A pressure canner and water bath canner**. These tools

will be *indispensable* for storing items bought in bulk or harvested from the garden. If you are canning, some other helpful things to have are funnels and a jar lifter. I bought my funnel and lifter in a kit that also came with a magnetic lid-picker-upper.

2. **Mason jars** of various sizes for canning, storing dried goods (they keep out moisture AND rodents), fermenting and sprouting.

3. **Meat slicer**: for making lunchmeat out of those Christmas hams.

4. **Cookie sheets or food dehydrator** for drying foods. I lay out herbs on a cookie sheet and dry them in our gas oven, turned off. The pilot light provides enough warmth to dry herbs. I also have a dehydrator for drying fruits, mushrooms, etc.

How to Save Up for High Dollar Items

I am not a fan of keeping one million kitchen gadgets around, but sometimes investing in good tools will help you save a LOT of money and a lot of time (which is essentially money). It might seem overwhelming to save $100.00 for canning supplies or $500.00 on a blender. That's okay. You can use the same saving principle we used for bulk buying.

Start with some seed money for another area in the budget (clothing is a good category to take from). I would start with just

$10.00. This is enough to buy a lot of entry-level gadgets at Goodwill; knives, garlic mincers, potato peelers, funnels, etc.

There are two ways to fund your envelope for larger purchases. One way is to reserve just $5.00-$10.00 per month (or more) from your food budget and put it into the cooking tools envelope. You could also go with a percentage- 5% - 20%, perhaps. Within a few months of saving, you'll be able to purchase a water bath canner.

The second way to fund your cooking tools envelope is to save money by using them. Perhaps you have foraged some free raspberries or mulberries, for example. Make jelly or jam with the fruit. Then calculate how much money you have saved by preserving the free food.

If you've made 10 half-pint jars of jam, you've saved about $8.00 (after costs of sugar, pectin, etc.). If your family goes through one half-pint per week, the jam will last two and a half months. The money that you DON'T spend on jam can be put into the cooking tools envelope.

Note: If you save money by buying in bulk AND using your tools (for example, canning peaches that you bought on sale), the savings will have to go in one envelope or another; not both. If you have most of the tools you need, put MORE money into the bulk buying fund and LESS into the cooking tools fund. Likewise, if you have a lot of money in the bulk buying fund and would rather save for a special gadget, move some of that money into the cooking tools fund.

How to Pick a Gadget

If you are going to buy a new kitchen tool, try to find something that will save you money in the long run. For example, if you have the resources to make your own sausage for free, invest in a sausage stuffer. If you would like to start making your own wines with free fruit, invest in an airlock. There are many small cooking devices that will save money, but there are also fancy vegetable slicers, wire whisks, or cookie cutters that won't save any money at all, though they might make cooking more fun. Try to determine the difference between a real investment (something that will generate a return) and a toy.

Tips for Easy Meal Prep

There are several things you can do to make meal prep easier.

1. **Utilize batch cooking**. When I make rice, chop potatoes or cook ground beef, I make enough for the entire week. Instead of making a small pot of rice for every meal, I make a large pot for my first rice meal on Monday and then store the rest in the fridge to use for all other rice meals throughout the week. I try to do this with every food ingredient that I possibly can. Most any vegetables that you need to cut up- onions or carrots, for example, can all be cut up at once. Later in the week when things get busy, you will only have to *assemble* meals, not prepare them from scratch. You can read more about this in the food prep ideas section below.

2. **Start cooking the most time-consuming items first**. For example, if your meal includes pasta, start boiling water before cooking the ground beef and heating up sauce. If you start with the sauce and then start the pasta after that, your meal will take twice as long to prepare. Likewise, if your meal includes vegetables that need to be cooked (like potatoes or corn on the cob), start those things <u>first</u> and do shorter tasks while the potatoes are cooking.

3. **Cut up vegetables & fruits before you preserve them**. For example, when I freeze peppers from the garden, I make long

slices to use for stir fry and fajitas, and I dice up the ends into small squares for pizza topping. Then I freeze the slices in one gallon size bag (so I can just grab a handful to use and then close the bag and pop it back into the freezer) and the smaller pieces in another smaller bag.

4. **Use pressure canned meat and beans**. This can save a LOT of cooking time. With a pressure canner, your food is cooked AND preserved at the same time, instead of cooking in one step (for example, cooking beans in a slow cooker) and preserving in another (putting the beans in plastic bags and freezing them). The other major time/sanity saver with pressure canned foods is that they require no time to thaw.

Weekly Food Prep Ideas

Ideally, you should have a food prep time once a week, where you slice, dice, and make staples (like yogurt or bread) for the entire week. In reality though, I find that I do one or two food prep tasks every weekday. There's no reason to make more cheese when there is still some left from last week! Still, it's good to keep a running list of food prep that can be done when you have the time.

Doing your own cutting, slicing and cooking saves money, but it can also take some time. Having a weekly food prep session can save time, and also dirties fewer dishes in the process. Instead of using the chef's knife and cutting board for every meal,

I use it a couple times in the same day, simply rinsing it off between items (I use separate cutting boards for meat and vegetables).

Here are some food prep tasks you can do once a week to save time:

1. **Chop onions**. When you chop, chop almost the whole bag. Put your weekly allotment of chopped onions in a container in the fridge and freeze the rest. Now you won't have to chop for another month or so. Hint: I chop onions in my blender. You can do the same, or if you don't have a powerful blender you can use a food processor.

2. **Mince garlic**. When you mince, mince several bulbs at once. Store the mincings in a small jar, covered with olive oil. Hint: I use a special garlic mincer tool to make the job easier.

3. **Freeze extra broth**. When I make soups, I use the gelatinous broth that comes out of a jar of canned bone-in chicken. If I'm just using the chicken and not the broth, however, I will strain off the broth and freeze it for another time.

4. **Boil eggs**. Turn on a pot of water and boil enough eggs for the entire week. Boiled eggs keep longer with the shell intact, though, so don't peel them unless you are going to use them in the next day or two.

5. **Cook extra rice**. I always cook a week's worth of rice at

once. I start cooking it before our first rice meal of the week (stir-fry). It takes a little longer to cook 3x as much, so I start a little earlier. When the rice is done cooking before lunch, I dump some of it into the pan of stir-fry, but the rest goes into a container for the fridge. Whenever I need rice for a meal, I just scoop it out of the container.

6. **Cook a whole pound (or two) of bacon**. Before cooking, use a pair of scissors to cut the slices into small 1/2" pieces. When it is done cooking, you will have "bacon bits" that you can put in the freezer in meal-sized quantities. I use bacon bits for pizza, soup, quiche/omelets, baked potatoes and more.

7. **Sausage or other lunch meat**: prepare the same way as you would bacon, frying up a whole pound (or two!) and freezing in smaller portions to use as accents to a meal. I have done this with sausage, pepperoni, sliced ham, and other more expensive meats that I don't buy or use regularly.

8. **Brown enough meat for several days**. Then keep it in the fridge, next to the rice, and scoop out as much as is needed. I usually have one or two "meats of the week". I might thaw and cook a pound of ground beef on Monday, and use that for meals until I run out on Thursday. Then I might get out a jar of canned chicken or lamb, and use that for the rest of the week. This helps cut down on meat waste, because you are using up the whole container before you get out any new meat, as opposed to having a chicken breast meal for lunch, ground beef for dinner, etc., and then having a bunch of rotten raw meat leftovers in the fridge on

Sunday. If I run out of "meat of the week" and only need enough for one meal, I will pull out leftover cooked meat from the freezer, or use frozen pre-cooked ham/sausage/pepperoni to accent the meal.

There are a lot of other things you can do once a week on food prep day. These are not limited to chopping, slicing and boiling, but also include making dairy products, baking different breads, shredding cheese and more. I have included some of these ideas (with recipes) in my book *Pizza Night; a Simple Meal Plan*.

2-in-1 Meals: Cooking Only Once A Day

There are many time-saving strategies out there for home cooks. I love the idea of crock-pot freezer meals in particular, but I think it is a waste of time to assemble a meal, freeze it, take it out and wash the bag/box you froze it in. Most of my ingredients are prepared ready-to-cook before they go into food storage. For example, if I'm freezing or canning carrots, they will be peeled and chopped beforehand.

Utilizing the Crock Pot

At 11:30-12:00 noon (depending on when you eat lunch), assemble lunch. If you have done the prep work (chopping, slicing, browning) earlier in the week, this should be simple and fast- no longer than 15-20 minutes. After you are done, assemble another simple meal in the crock pot. Before you sit down to eat lunch, plug in the crockpot. Doing a crock pot meal in the evening eliminates the need to stop your afternoon project just to make supper. It will also ensure that there is ALWAYS dinner made.

If you aren't home for lunch, do your meal assembly in the morning before work or school. Lunch will be sandwiches, wraps or leftovers, and dinner will be a crock pot meal. You may have to set the pot on "low" instead of high if it is going to be cooking all day long.

Toward the end of this book, I have included some frugal crock pot recipes for you to try. Some of the recipes make enough for two or three meals, which you can freeze and cook later.

Cooking With Flavor Families

Flavor Families: A Frugal Cook's Best Friend

Cooking is really not as hard as it sounds. "Throwing together a meal" or "winging it" or "eyeballing it" without a recipe is not as hard as it sounds either, if you use the concept of *flavor families.*

In order to eat for $10.00 per week, you must be very, very flexible with your recipes. My family does not eat according to the weekly meal plan; we do not even eat according to sales or coupons. We eat according to what is in the pantry or freezer. We don't buy special ingredients for a single meal. All ingredients must be multi-purpose. What I have realized is that most ingredients ARE multi-purpose. It just takes skill to prepare these basic foods in appealing ways.

Lamb Tastes Terrible... Or Does It?

Last year, we bought a lamb at the 4-H livestock auction. The lamb was not a good fit for our hobby farm, so we decided to butcher it. We put some of the roasts in the freezer, and canned all of the ground meat. Not knowing any better, I used some of the ground meat in spaghetti sauce. It was awful! It tasted very gamey, and the flavor just did not mesh with the tomato sauce at all.

As you can imagine, we were very disappointed. Here we had just put an entire lamb into the pantry, and it tasted terrible. Because we still had so much meat, I felt compelled to use it up. Desperate, I took out my copy of *The Professional Chef* and tried to find recipes for lamb.

I discovered that all of the recipes for lamb used the same four or five herbs and spices. Reading further about lamb, I found out that it is one of the main meats eaten in the Middle East, and therefore was commonly cooked with Middle Eastern spices.

The next time I cooked the awful ground lamb, I did not use a tomato based sauce. Instead, I fried up the lamb and added onions, chili powder and cumin. I made a yogurt/dill/cilantro sauce, and served the lamb and sauce on discount pita bread like a sandwich. It was WONDERFUL! I could not believe how good my lamb tasted. It was not bad meat- it was just that I was using a mismatched flavor family.

Notice that I did not have to run to the store in order to buy special ingredients for the lamb. I used spices I already had, herbs from my garden, and pita bread from the pantry. It wasn't my supplies that were lacking; it was my skills.

How to Build a Meal

Using the flavor families as a guideline, this is how I plan a meal.

1. Start with the **protein and carbohydrate** you will be using for the meal. For example, let's pretend I have ground beef and rice to use. Some good flavor families for rice and beef are Asian, Middle Eastern, or Latin American.

2. Use the **vegetable** you are serving to further determine which flavor family would be best. If I am using sweet peppers as the vegetable, that eliminates Asian and Middle Eastern cuisines.

3. Find a meal template that works for the flavor family you have chosen. Some of my meal templates are stir fry, pasta & sauce, tacos, sandwiches, crock pot roast (any chunk of meat cooked in the crock pot), rice with sauce, hash, pizza, soup, or casserole. These are the types of meals that I've outlined in my book, *Pizza Night; a Simple Meal Plan*. For my Latin American meal with rice, ground beef and peppers, I've decided to make a hash meal with fried onions and bell peppers (fajita style) and a fried egg.

4. Use **spices and/or fruit and dairy** to finish off the meal in the flavor family you have chosen. For my fajita rice I will use taco seasoning as the main flavoring. On the side I'll serve sour cream, queso blanco, and salsa. If I had an avocado or other Latin American fruit, I would serve that as well. If those items are not

already in my pantry, I won't serve them.

A List of Flavor Family Ideas

A flavor family is simply ingredients that go well together. I like to classify these by nationality, but you can experiment and make up your own flavor families. Some ideas are Italian, French, Latin American, Middle Eastern, Asian, or subcategories of "American"; Southeastern, Hawaiian, Midwestern, etc. I've included an extended list in Appendix B: Flavor Families at the end of this book to inspire you. If you find a list that includes a lot of your pantry ingredients, start learning a little more about the culture and "cooking like the locals".

How Flavor Families Can Help

Of course there are many more flavor families than those listed in the appendix, but I think they will give you a good start. The lists will help you with the following:

1. What to do with those random weird ingredients that you got on sale.

2. How to cook chicken (or another common staple ingredient) 10 different ways. You may also find some ingredients on the list that you didn't know were even food items (like purslane or fiddlehead ferns).

My hope is that flavor families open your mind to a world of cooking possibilities, using the deals and steals that are already in your pantry.

Clean Up Tricks

Lastly, we want to save time, money and sanity by cleaning up efficiently.

1. When you heat milk, rinse the pan in cold water to prevent sticking.

2. Always heat a skillet before you add oil or butter; the food will stick less. This works especially well with cast iron.

3. Use salt and oil to wash a pan that has something sticky burned to the bottom of it.

4. Rinse dishes if you are not washing them right away. This will get the big chunks of food off before they dry onto your dishes.

5. Let every family member have his or her own cup, and only wash those once a day. Cups hardly get dirty enough to justify washing them more than that.

6. Use cloth napkins. Give each diner their own cloth napkin and napkin ring. When the meal is over, the napkin goes right back in the ring unless it is too dirty to use again. Depending on how many people are in your family, using cloth napkins can save between $5.00 and $25.00 per year, and it is not much more work than disposable napkins. I do keep disposable napkins on

hand for my husband, who prefers them, but I still put a cloth napkin at his place setting and sometimes he actually uses it.

7. Use wash cloths instead of paper towels to wipe down counters. There are special drying racks that you can mount above your sink (or elsewhere) to dry wet wash clothes that have been used, but rinsed out. If you dry wash clothes in between uses, they will not stink like those left wet in the sink.

8. Use a jar brush and rubber gloves to wash dishes. The jar brush will save a lot of time, especially if you do a lot of canning, and the gloves will save your hands if you do a lot of dishes. The gloves will also allow you to wash in hotter water, which cuts down on drying time and time spent adjusting the water temperature.

9. Hang a kitchen towel off one of your cabinets or over the oven door handle. Use this towel to dry your hands whenever they are wet. This will cut down on a lot of mess.

10. Give scraps to chickens, or put them in the compost pile. This cuts down on waste and helps keep the trash can empty.

Part 3: Planning

It's time to put all that we've learned into practice! This last section is for the Planners out there, and includes some tips on how to choose different meals for your family, as well as Appendix A: Frugal Recipes, and Appendix B: Flavor Families, to help you create a flexible menu that works.

Cooking Method Considerations

As you design some of your template meals, carefully chose your cooking method. Use the following criteria to pick the best method.

1. How much electricity/propane does it use?

The most efficient electrical device you can use to cook with is an electric pressure cooker, called an instant pot (or something like that). Second in line is probably the microwave, then crock pot, then stovetop. The most expensive way to cook something is in the oven.

Oven tips: You can save on oven electricity usage by cooking two or more things at once. For example, when I bake things for farmers market, I do all of the 365 degree recipes at once. Then I turn up the heat and bake all items that need to be cooked at 375 degrees, then 400 degrees. In addition, you can turn off the oven after most of the cooking is done, and it will still cook. Don't believe me? Try leaving fully-baked cookies in the oven when it is turned off but still hot. I don't think you'll like the results!

Preheating time can be eliminated if you are baking something that takes several hours to cook.

Stovetop tips: Match pots and pans to burner size. Using a

small pan for a large burner is a waste of energy. Use lids that fit on your pots, and always boil water with the lid on. It heats up faster that way.

2. How much time does it take?

Like I mentioned in Part 2: Cooking, I try to spend as little time in the kitchen as possible. As a housewife, I already spend time cooking every day. I want things to be as fast and as efficient as possible so I can do other fun things.

I prefer to cook dinner meals in the crock pot, and lunch meals on the stove. Breakfast is also on the stove or made ahead of time (yogurt and granola).

3. How many dishes does it take?

Though time-convenient and relatively economical in electricity usage, the stove top method of cooking uses a lot of dishes. A pot or two to cook things with, a fork to stir, and lids. In addition to spending more time doing dishes, I also spend more time cleaning up spill-overs and food that has crusted onto the stove top.

Menu Troubleshooting

"I have a lot of cheap food in my pantry from sales and bulk buying, but I never use it. Instead I end up paying full price for items that I know I will use."

There may be some discrepancies between what you are buying and what you are cooking. Ask yourself the following:

1. Are bargain-bin, bottom-dollar pantry foods part of a different flavor family than you are currently cooking with? If certain canned foods or spice mixes have been in your pantry for years, they are not part of the flavor families in your recipe repertoire. To remedy the situation, you can either 1) cook meals from flavor family that fits the unused ingredient, or 2) toss the ingredient and don't buy any more. <u>Only buy ingredients you know you will use.</u>

2. Are you cooking "like mom did" even though your situation is different than mom's? The family meal heritage is more deeply embedded than you might think! I began to realize this after my now-husband and I started dating. I grew up eating lots of frozen meat, butter, cheese, pasta, bread and frozen veggies, but very few desserts. We were a typical American farm family. Meat and milk were plentiful. My mom was busy helping with the farm business and also working a part-time job, so oftentimes we kids or my dad would cook. The meals were very simple and seldom were there desserts.

My husband, on the other hand, grew up in an Amish family where mom and sisters made food (and lots of it!) for every meal. There were plenty of fruits and vegetables, and less meat compared to my family. Because they had no refrigeration, much of the food was canned, and baked goods and desserts were a staple. They had something sweet for every meal. Something called "coffee soup"- basically a huge pot of mocha served with saltine crackers- would be breakfast on Sunday morning.

Eventually I realized there were pros and cons to each diet. I saw that my family's diet was healthier, but since I didn't live on a farm anymore it was very expensive. Instead of using cheese and butter to flavor things, I learned how to use spices, sauces and seasonings. Through Hubs' family I learned that it's possible to pressure can practically anything, and it is cheaper and easier to use than frozen food. I try to take the best of both worlds and use it in my menu planning.

Consider your own situation. Are there meals that you make, or foods that you buy only "because mom did"? Do you still buy asparagus and rhubarb even though you now live in Florida? Perhaps you are like me and are still trying to flavor everything with cheese and butter when it would be easier and cheaper to use herbs and spices. I am still amazed at how cultural influences from even 150 years ago are still present in the way I cook now. After we got married, I was surprised at how similar my mother-in-law's cooking was to that of my Grandma. However, my grandma's family came from Germany just like my husband's

Amish ancestors did, back in the day. Meat, potatoes, apple pie. But in order to be a frugal cook, I must also learn how to utilize different flavor families than just the ones I grew up with.

3. Is your personal flavor <u>preference</u> different from that which is in your pantry? Perhaps you like pizza and pasta, but your pantry is full of home-grown beets or venison. To remedy this, you can either change your pantry items, or change your preference.

4. Does your flavor preference include expensive items that you cannot grow or make yourself? Your choice, again, is to either change your location or change your preference. The other alternative is to search for new flavor families that you might like.

5. Do you cook whatever the media is telling you to cook? Perhaps modern culture dictates a flavor family that you cannot afford. Why is it that "superfoods"- or, whatever the media is pushing- tend to be so expensive? If we listened to popular culture (and this includes the health community), we'd be making entire meals of grass-fed organic beef, coconut oil, avocados and almonds. Not exactly the cheapest items on the shelf.

Someday, our superfoods will go out of style and become just as cheap as the next thing. Think about bananas. Though common and cheap today, they were unknown to Americans until 1876. After that, they were sold individually wrapped in tin foil, at the cost of ten cents each- about an hour's wages. As they became more readily available and affordable to the average

American, bananas were marketed as a health food. Some advertisements called it an "all-food fruit" and others suggested that bananas could be used to replace meat in the diet of children. Hmm... does this remind you of what we have going on today? Instead of using bananas as meat though, we use almonds or coconuts to make milk and bread. Why, when it would be cheaper to buy real milk, or bread made with wheat? A frugal housewife knows that just because something is trendy does not mean that it is the right choice for her family. It takes wisdom to discern truth from marketing.

Meal Planning Worksheet

Before the week begins, pick out some basic meal templates (casserole, roast, soup, etc.) for each day. Sometimes I will also write which main ingredients I plan to use (meat, starch), but side dishes and seasonings are left "to be determined" until the day before or the day of the meal. If there are some days left blank, you can serve "frozen dinners" a.k.a. leftovers. When planning for the week, don't forget about any potlucks coming up or snacks that you would like to make. Then look over what you have written, and determine what food prep tasks would be necessary.

While I have a basic idea of what we will eat every week, I don't plan the *exact* details of the meal until the day before or the day of. You never know when someone will drop off a bag of vegetables that need to be used right away, or perhaps the pear tree will start producing half way through the week. The frugal meal planner is a flexible meal planner. You can download a printable version of this sheet on the "Printables and Downloads" page at www.therenaissancehousewife.com.

Food prep tasks this week:

Snacks to make this week:

Potluck meals to make this week:

Weekday Breakfasts:

Saturday Breakfast:

Sunday Breakfast:

Monday Lunch:

Monday Dinner:

Tuesday Lunch:

Tuesday Dinner:

Wednesday Lunch:

Wednesday Dinner:

Thursday Lunch:

Thursday Dinner:

Friday Lunch:

Friday Dinner:

Saturday Lunch:

Saturday Dinner:

Sunday Lunch:

Sunday Dinner:

Appendix A: Frugal Recipes

Crock Pot Dinners

Many oven or stove top recipes can be converted to be cooked in a crock pot. Here are some tips for adapting your own recipes:

1. A slow cooker retains moisture. While this is fantastic for tender and juicy meats, it does not work so well for breads or food that needs to dry while they are being cooked.

2. Allow enough cooking time on the low setting. One of my most-repeated mistakes as a new housewife was making crock pot meals for lunch. I always forgot to put the ingredients in at an early hour, and the vegetables would still be hard at lunch. This is why I mostly do crock pot meals for dinner, now.

3. Milk or sour cream should be added after the food is done cooking, in most cases, in order to prevent curdling.

4. Vegetables do not need to be browned or sautéed before they are put in the slow cooker.

5. If the oven/stove top recipe says cook for 15-30 minutes, you will need to cook it in the crock pot for 1 1/2- 2 1/2 hours on high, or 4 to 8 hours on low in the crock pot. For

recipes that call for 35-40 minutes of cooking, do 3 to 4 hours on high or 6 to 10 hours on low. For recipes that call for 50 minutes to 3 hours of cooking time, do 4 to 6 hours on high or 8 to 18 hours on low. Uncooked meat and vegetable combinations will require at least 8 hours on low.

Frugal Meals to Get You Started

Below are several slow-cooker meals that will feed four people for a minimum amount of money. I have picked these meals in particular because they use inexpensive, healthy ingredients. Most do not include bouillon cubes, cream soups or other heavily processed ingredients.

All of these four-person meals are very doable on the $20.00 per person, per week "beginner budget". To meet the $10.00 budget, though, the meals will require several ingredients to be homemade, grown in a garden, or purchased at a discount. You do not *have to* use homemade ingredients for these recipes, but it will make the meals even less expensive.

Note about bell peppers: Some of these recipes call for bell peppers. This is a very costly vegetable to purchase fresh at the grocery store. If you can, grow your own bell peppers in a raised bed garden (that's the easiest), buy them on sale, frozen, or otherwise discounted. If you don't, the cost of a single green pepper will probably put the meal over $2.00.

If you want, you can use celery as an alternative for bell peppers. It may change the flavor a bit, but is certainly much cheaper.

Note about cooking wines and broth: you can also

substitute broth for cooking wine in recipes that call for it. Because I pressure can bone-in meat, I have plenty of free broth to use. Cooking wine, on the other hand, costs money. On a low budget, it's smart to cut corners wherever you can.

Beef Recipes:

Stuffed Cabbage

12 large cabbage leaves
1 lb. ground beef
1/2 cup cooked rice
1/2 tsp. salt
1/8 tsp pepper
1/4 tsp. leaf thyme
1/4 tsp. nutmeg
1/4 tsp. cinnamon
6 oz. (1 can) tomato paste
3/4 c. water

Boil 4 cups water. Turn heat off, and soak leaves in water for 5 minutes. Remove, drain and cool. Combine remaining ingredients (except tomato paste and water). Place 2 TB of mixture on each leaf and roll firmly. Stack in slow cooker. Combine tomato paste and water, and pour over stuffed cabbage. Cover and cook on low for 8 to 10 hours.

Beef Stew

2 lbs. stew beef, cut into 1 1/2" cubes*

1 c. onion, finely chopped

2 ½ c. cubed peeled & cubed potatoes

2 carrots, peeled and sliced

10 oz. beans, cooked

2 cloves minced garlic

1 sweet green pepper, seeded and cut into strips**

2 tsp. dried parsley flakes***

1/2 c. beef broth

2 tsp. paprika

1 tsp. salt

16 oz. canned whole tomatoes**

*I always use canned stew meat; typically venison.

**Only use home grown peppers- otherwise omit this ingredient. Tomatoes are much cheaper grown at home, as well.

***A free alternative to parsley flakes is dehydrated kale from the garden. You can also dehydrate local greens (chickweed or lambsquarter, for example) to use in place of dried parsley.

Place all ingredients except broth, paprika, salt and tomatoes into crock pot. Mix reserved ingredients, pour over top of pot contents and stir to blend. Cover and cook on low 10 to 12 hours or on high for 5 to 6 hours.

Meatloaf

This makes enough for two meals, so make two loaves and freeze the second. As always, you can substitute almost any ground meat for the ground beef.

 8 oz. (1 can) tomato sauce*
 1 egg
 1/2 cup chopped onion
 1/2 cup chopped sweet green pepper*
 1/3 cup dry seasoned bread crumbs*
 1/2 tsp. garlic salt
 1/4 tsp black pepper
 1 1/2 lbs. ground beef
 1 c. ketchup
 1/4 c. brown sugar

 *Use homegrown or homemade ingredients.

Reserve 1/3 c. of tomato sauce and mix with ketchup and brown sugar. Set aside. In mixing bowl, combine remaining sauce and egg. Stir in onion, green pepper, bread crumbs, garlic salt, and black pepper. Add ground beef and mix well. Divide in two parts. Line crock pot with plastic wrap or tin foil, and put in one half of the mixture. Shape like a loaf, filling out the inside of the cooker. Then pull the loaf shape out of the pot and freeze for later. Put the other half of your meatloaf mixture in the empty crock pot, once again pressing to fill out the corners and mold into a loaf-like shape. Pour the ketchup/brown sugar sauce over the top of the loaf. Cook for 8 to 10 hours on low, or 4 to 6 hours on high. Insert meat thermometer into center of loaf. When the temperature reads 170 degrees Fahrenheit, the meatloaf is done.

To use the frozen meatloaf, remove the wrapping and place inside empty slow cooker. For best results, thaw the meatloaf inside the slow cooker insert, in the fridge, overnight until you are ready to cook it the next day. You will need to mix up a second batch of topping sauce. If I don't have a jar of tomato sauce already open, I will just use 1 1/3 cups of ketchup with 1/4 cup of brown sugar. Top the thawed meatloaf with this new sauce, and cook according to directions above.

Beef Fajitas

If you don't have a good source of cheap beef, use venison or chicken in this recipe. It makes 12 servings; enough to freeze or use for tomorrow's lunch.

1 1/2 lbs. beef steak*
1 cup sliced onion
1 green sweet pepper, sliced
1 jalapeno pepper, chopped
1 TB cilantro
2 cloves garlic or 1/4 tsp garlic powder
1 tsp. chili powder
1 tsp. ground cumin
1 tsp. coriander
1/2 tsp. salt
8 oz. (1 can) chopped tomatoes
*I would use a quart jar of canned chunk meat. That way you don't have to shred the meat before it is served.
Toppings: sour cream, guacamole, shredded cheese, salsa. You will also need some tortillas for this meal.

Cut flank steak into 6 portions. In the slow cooker, combine meat, onion, green sweet pepper, jalapeno pepper, cilantro, garlic, chili powder, cumin, coriander, and salt. Add tomatoes. Cover and cook on low for 8 to 10 hours or on high for 4 to 5 hours. Remove the meat from the crock pot and shred. Return meat to the crock pot and stir.

BBQ Beef

When done, this will make enough for 12 servings. It could make a nice potluck/party dish, or you can freeze whatever is left over to use later.

3 lbs. boneless chuck roast (you can use any type of beef (besides ground beef) for this recipe, including canned.
1 1/2 c. ketchup
2 TB mustard
1/4 c. packed brown sugar
1/4 cup red wine vinegar
2 TB Worcestershire sauce
1 tsp. liquid smoke flavoring
1/2 tsp. salt
1/4 tsp. pepper
1/4 tsp. garlic powder

Note: you can also use three cups of store bought barbecue sauce in replacement of all ingredients after the chuck roast. Whether you use homemade or store bought sauce will depend on the price of each.

Put chuck roast in the slow cooker and combine remaining ingredients into a bowl. Pour sauce mixture over chuck roast. Cover and cook on low for 8 to 10 hours, or 4 to 5 hours on high. When the meat is done cooking, remove and shred for sandwiches. Put the meat back into the pot and stir back into the sauce until it is completely coated. Spoon meat onto bread for sandwiches.

Sloppy Joes

This recipe makes enough for two meals, so be sure to freeze the extra. Ground venison or pork makes a good substitute for ground beef if you can't find any in your price range.

3 pounds ground beef
1 c. chopped onion
2 cloves minced garlic or 1/4 tsp. garlic powder
1 1/2 c. ketchup
1 cup chopped sweet green pepper*
1/2 c. water
1/4 c. brown sugar
1/4 c. mustard
1/4 c. vinegar
1/4 c. Worcestershire sauce
1 TB chili powder

*Use homegrown peppers; otherwise omit this ingredient or replace with celery.
Serve with hamburger buns.

Brown ground beef in skillet with onion and garlic. Drain off fat (save and use for another purpose). In the slow cooker, combine remaining ingredients and then stir in the meat mixture. Cook on low for 6 to 8 hours, or on high for 3 to 4 hours.

Poultry Recipes:

Turkey and Corn Casserole

1 onion, chopped
1 can/pint corn
4 large eggs
1/2 c. evaporated milk
1/3 c. flour
Salt & black pepper to taste
2 c. cooked, chopped turkey*
1 c. shredded cheese

*Turkey goes on sale around Thanksgiving. You can cook one or two birds, and then save the cooked meat in the freezer for easy meals like this.

Mix all ingredients (except turkey and cheese) and pour into in lightly greased slow cooker. Stir in turkey chunks. Cover and cook on high for 2 1/2 to 3 hours or until knife inserted comes out clean. Sprinkle casserole with cheese; cover and cook until the cheese is melted (about 15 minutes) and serve immediately.

Chicken Enchiladas

2 lbs. chopped cooked chicken*
1 can (4 1/2 oz.) chopped mild green chilies**
1 onion, chopped
1 pint/can enchilada sauce**
Corn tortillas
Shredded cheese

*I like to use canned chicken because it is already cooked. You can reserve the broth for another recipe.
** Make or grow these items yourself.

Stir together chicken, chilies, onion and 1 cup of enchilada sauce. Dip corn tortilla into remaining enchilada sauce and place in the bottom of the slow cooker. Spread 3 TB of chicken mixture on wet tortilla and sprinkle with cheese. Keep layering tortillas, chicken and cheese until you've reached the top of the pot. The last layer should be a sprinkle of cheese. Pour any extra enchilada sauce over the top of the tortilla stack. Cook on low 4 to 6 hours or on high for 1 1/2 to 2 1/2 hours.

Tostada Pie

2 tsp. oil
2 lb. cooked chicken*
2 tsp. chili powder
1 tsp. ground cumin
1 1/2 c. chopped onion
1 tsp. salt
2 cloves garlic, minced, or 1/4 tsp. garlic powder
1 can/pint tomato sauce**
8 corn tortillas
Butter and shredded cheese
Optional: sour cream and green onions*

*Again, I like to use canned chicken here because it is already cooked.
** Use homemade or home grown ingredients to help with the cost.

Sauté onion, chicken, chili powder, cumin, salt, and garlic in a pan with oil. Stir in tomato sauce. Lightly butter one of the tortillas and place in the bottom of the pot (buttered side down). Spread with meat sauce and a sprinkle of cheese. Keep on layering tortillas, meat sauce and cheese until everything is used up, ending with a sprinkle of cheese. Cover and cook on high for 1 hour. When done, cut into wedges and serve with optional toppings.

Pork Recipes:

Pork, Potato and Green Bean Stew

This recipe serves 8.

1 quart chicken broth
1 lb. boneless pork loin, trimmed of fat and cut into pieces
4 potatoes, cut into 1/2" cubes
1 onion, chopped
2 cloves garlic, minced
1/3 c. flour
2 cups frozen green beans*
2 tsp. Worcestershire sauce
1/2 tsp. thyme
1/2 tsp. black pepper

*Grow it yourself for a cheaper meal.

Heat pork loin, potatoes, onion, and garlic with half of the chicken broth in a skillet for 5 to 10 minutes over medium heat. Transfer to slow cooker. Combine 3/4 cup chicken broth and flour in a small bowl and set aside. Add remaining broth, beans, Worcestershire sauce, thyme and pepper to crock pot and stir. Cover and cook 8 to 10 hours on low, or 4 to 5 hours on high. When finished cooking, stir in flour mixture and cook 30 minutes on high.

German Potato Soup

This may make enough for two meals, so keep a freezer container handy.

    1/2 lb. bacon, cooked in bits*
    1 onion, chopped
    2 carrots, peeled and diced
    1 c. chopped cabbage
    1/4 c. chopped parsley**
    4 c. beef broth
    1 lb. potatoes, washed and diced
    1 bay leaf
    2 tsp. black pepper
    1 tsp. salt
    1/2 tsp. caraway seeds
    1/4 tsp. nutmeg
    1/2 c. sour cream

*For a more frugal meal, cut the bacon in half, replace with a smaller amount of ham, or omit entirely, using a little bit of bacon grease instead for flavor.
**Any wild green will work in replacement of parsley.

Combine onion, carrots, cabbage, parsley, broth and potatoes in slow cooker. Stir in seasonings. Cover and cook on low for 8 to 10 hours, or on high for 4 to 5 hours. Remove bay leaf. Lastly, stir in bacon pieces and sour cream before serving.

Pork Roast

1 large onion, sliced
2 1/2 lbs. boneless pork loin roast
1 c. hot water
1/4 c. white sugar
3 TB red wine vinegar
2 TB soy sauce
1 tsp. ketchup
1/2 tsp. black pepper
1/2 tsp. salt
1/4 tsp. garlic powder
1 dash hot pepper sauce, or to taste

Arrange onion slices evenly over the bottom of the slow cooker, and then place the roast on top of the onion. In a bowl, mix together water, sugar, vinegar, soy sauce, ketchup, black pepper, salt, garlic powder, and hot sauce; pour over roast. Cover and cook on Low for 6 to 8 hours, or on High for 3 to 4 hours.

Vegetarian Recipes:

Vegetable Cheese Soup

1 lb. corn
1 c. shopped, peeled potatoes
1 c. chopped carrots
1/2 c. chopped onions
1 tsp. celery seed
1/2 tsp black pepper
1 quart vegetable or chicken broth
1 cup shredded or process cheese

Combine corn, potatoes, carrots, onions, celery seed and black pepper in slow cooker. Add broth and cook on Low for 8 to 10 hours or High for 4 to 5 hours. After cooking, gently stir in cheese and cook until it is melted (if you have been cooking on the low setting, turn it up on high for the last 20 to 30 minutes).

French Onion Soup

3 lbs. sliced onions
1/2 c. melted butter*
6-8 slices of French bread, cubed
4-5 c. chicken broth
Salt to taste

*For a cheaper version, use oil or animal fat instead of butter.

Place sliced onions in slow cooker; pour in butter and mix to coat onions thoroughly. Stir in cubed bread. Add chicken broth to cover; stir well. Cover and cook on Low for 10 to 18 hours or on High for 4 to 5 hours, stirring occasionally. Stir well during the last hour.

Baked Potatoes

5-7 medium potatoes
Toppings: butter, salt, sour cream, bacon bits, cheese, fresh chives or green onions.

Scrub potatoes and place into the slow cooker. I like to add some water- ¼ to ½ cup- in the bottom for tenderness. Cook on Low for 8 hours or on High for 4 to 6 hours.

Two-Bean Corn Chili

1 pint/can black eyed peas*
1 pint/can navy beans*
1 onion, chopped
1/2 c. tomato paste
1 cup water
2 tsp. chili powder
1/2 tsp. ground cumin
1/4 tsp. oregano
1 tsp. mustard
1 c. corn
1/2 c. chopped scallions*
1/4 c. diced chili or jalapeno peppers*
1 c. canned tomatoes*

*If you can grow and/or can these items yourself, the meal will be a lot cheaper.

Combine all ingredients in crock pot. Cover and cook on Low for 8 to 10 hours or on High for 4 to 5 hours.

Other Crock Pot Recipes:

Cinnamon Baked Apples

5 c. sliced, cored apples (4 medium)
2 TB c. butter melted
1 TB lemon juice
1/3 c. packed brown sugar
1 tsp. ground cinnamon
2 TB apple cider*

*If you don't have cider, use 1 TB apple cider vinegar with 1 TB water, or substitute another fruit juice.

Grease crock pot insert with cooking spray. In slow cooker, mix apples, butter and lemon juice. Sprinkle with brown sugar and cinnamon; toss to coat. Pour cider over apples. Cover and cook on Low for 3 hours 30 minutes or until apples are tender.

Baked Oatmeal

4 c. quick cooking oats
3/4 c. brown sugar
1 TB baking powder
1 tsp. salt
2 eggs
2 c. milk
2 tsp vanilla extract
Toppings – milk, yogurt*, berries*, fruit*

*Use homemade or homegrown toppings only.

Whisk the ingredients, minus the toppings, together in a mixing bowl. Generously spray slow cooker with non-stick cooking spray. Pour the mixture into the slow cooker. Cover and cook on Low for 5 hours. Keep warm until ready to serve.

Polenta

This recipe makes enough for two meals. If you put leftovers in the fridge overnight, they will form a solid lump. The lump can be sliced like bread and fried in butter or oil, and used as a snack or side dish for a later meal.

> 2-4 TB butter, melted
> 1/4 tsp. paprika*
> Dash of cayenne pepper*
> 6 c. boiling water
> 2 c. cornmeal
> 1 tsp salt

*Exchange these spices for "sweet" ones like cinnamon, cloves, or nutmeg, and the polenta can be eaten hot like breakfast cereal. Assemble everything the night before, cook overnight on Low, and breakfast is ready in the morning. Simply add milk and sweetener to taste. This is one of my favorite frugal alternatives to Cream of Wheat.

Use half of the butter to lightly grease the crock pot. Add paprika and cayenne. Turn to high while measuring remaining ingredients. Add to crock pot with remaining melted butter and stir well. Cover and cook on Low for 6 to 9 hours or on High for 2 to 3 hours, stirring occasionally.

Other Frugal Recipes

Included below are some frugal meals that do not use a slow cooker.

Quiche
1 c. plain yogurt*
¼ c. water
2-3 eggs, slightly beaten
1 c. flour
½ c. grated cheese
¼ c. chopped, cooked meat
¼ c. chopped, cooked vegetables*
Seasoning to taste
*Use homemade or homegrown ingredients

Preheat oven to 425 degrees Fahrenheit. Mix all ingredients thoroughly. Pour into a greased 9-inch pie plate. Bake for 30 to 35 minutes until set.

Quiche Potato Crust
3 TB oil
3 cups coarsely shredded raw potato
Mix oil and potato together in pie pan. Press the grated potato into a pie-crust shape. Bake at 425 degrees Fahrenheit for 15 minutes or until just beginning to brown. Fill with egg filling and follow instructions for baking quiche.

Tomato Soup

1 6-oz. can of tomato paste

24 oz. milk (refill tomato paste can four times)

1 tsp. salt or to taste

1 tsp. celery seed

Put tomato paste in a small saucepan. Add milk using the can. Add the salt and celery seed. Cook on medium heat, stirring occasionally.

Appendix B: Flavor Families

United States

New England Flavors
Apples, beans, blueberries, corn, cranberries, fiddlehead ferns, squash; beef, venison; turkey; clams, cod, flounder, lobster, oysters; maple syrup, molasses. Examples of New England cooking: cured pork, corned beef, sweet & sour relishes, pickles, baked beans, warm spices; traditional Thanksgiving meal items.

Southeastern Flavors
Black-eyed peas, rice; apples, berries, green beans, broccoli, cherries, collards, corn, cucumbers, eggplant, figs, melons, okra, onions, peaches, pears, persimmons, potatoes, spinach, squash, tomatoes, turnip greens, turnips; bear, beef, goat crappie, ground hog, mutton, opossum, pork, raccoon, squirrel, veal, venison; chicken; bluegill, crabs, crawfish, flounder, mullet, oysters, scallops, shrimp, trout. Examples of Southeastern cooking: barbeque, sweet potato pie, peanut soup, bourbon.

Gulf Coast Flavors
Artichokes, black eyed peas, chicory, coconuts, cushan, figs, okra, pecans, persimmons, red beans, rice, sassafras leaves, sugarcane, sweet potatoes; beef, pork; chicken; alligator, catfish, conch, crawfish, frog legs, oysters, pompano, red snapper, shrimp, snails, turtle. Examples of

Gulf Coast cooking: island spice, rum, tropical fruits, jerk, roux sauces, gumbo.

Midwest & Southwest Flavors
Barley, beans, oats, sorghum, soybeans, wheat; apples, berries, cactus, chiles, corn, peaches, pears, plums, potatoes, summer squash, turnips, winter squash; beef, lamb, pork, rabbit; chicken; bass, trout. Examples of Midwest & Southeastern cooking: Sausage, beer, cheese, jerky, meat & potatoes, smoked meats. Southwest spices: cumin, coriander, cinnamon, onions, garlic, oregano, chilies.

Western Flavors
Apples, artichokes, berries, cherries, chiles, fennel, figs, garlic, grapes, hazelnuts, melons, olives, onions, pears, pistachios, tomatoes, zucchini; beef, lamb; clams, crabs, oysters, salmon, saltwater fish. Examples of Western cooking: fresh fruits & vegetables, light sauces, and fish.

Alaskan Flavors
Barley, oats, rye, winter wheat; blueberries, cabbage, gooseberries, huckleberries, kale, raspberries, root vegetables, strawberries; caribou, elk, moose, reindeer, venison; dungeness crab, halibut, king crab, salmon. Examples of Alaskan cooking: sourdough, coffee & tea, fish, pot roasts, stews, potatoes, fruit pies.

Hawaiian Flavors
Rice, arrowroot, avocados, bananas, breadfruit, citrus, coconuts, guava, lychee, macadamia nuts, mangos, papaya,

passion fruit, pineapples, sugarcane, tamarind, taro, yams; chicken; bonito, crab, flounder, shrimp, swordfish, tuna. Examples of Hawaiian cooking: stir-fry, kimchee, adobo stews, fish stews, bean dishes.

International

Latin American Flavors

<u>Herbs & Spices</u>: Achiote, avocado leaves, banana leaves, cilantro, epazote, hoja santa, Mexican oregano, piloncillo.

<u>Meats, poultry & fish</u>: Beef, cavy (guinea pig), goat, lamb, llama, pork, rabbit, chicken, duck, turkey, mussels, salmon, sea bass, shrimp, snapper, squid.

<u>Grains, Beans & Nuts</u>: Amaranth, black beans, cacao, kidney beans, maize, peanuts, pecans, pepitas (pumpkin seeds), pinto beans, rice, quinoa, sesame seeds.

Tubers & Squash: Arracacha, cassava, chayote, jicama, malanga, potatoes, pumpkins, squash blossoms, sweet potatoes, taro, yucca.

<u>Vegetables</u>: Broccoli, cactus paddles (nopalitos), chard, chilies, corn, eggplant, kale, lettuce, okra, onions, spinach, sweet peppers, tomatillos, tomatoes, turnips, zucchini.

<u>Fruits</u>: Avocados, bananas, breadfruit, cherimoya, grapes, guanabana guava, kiwi, limes, mangos, oranges,

papaya, pineapples, plums, prickly pears, quince, tamarind.

Dairy: Crema, goat cheese, queso anejo, queso chihuahua, queso fresco, queso ranchero.

Chinese Flavors

Grains: barley, corn, millet, rice, sorghum (gaoling), wheat.

Staple ingredients: Millet, rice, soybean, wheat.

General flavors: Garlic, ginger, green onions, soy sauce.

Condiments & cooking liquids: Bean sauce, broad bean paste, chili paste, Chinese rice vinegar (white, red, and black), duck sauce, hoisin sauce, hot bean paste, oyster sauce, plum sauce, rice wine, salted black beans, sesame oil, sesame paste, soy sauce, sweet-salty sauce.

Seasonings: Anise seeds, chiles, cinnamon, dried shrimp, fennel seeds, fermented black beans, five-spice powder, garlic, ginger, green onions, star anise, Szechwan pepper (fagara)

Fresh, Dried, and Pickled: Adzuki beans, bamboo shoots, bean sprouts (mung & soybean), carrots, Chinese broccoli, Chinese cabbage (bok choy), Chinese celery, chrysanthemum greens, daikon radishes, dried black mushrooms, dried citrus peel (orange and tangerine), dried fungus (cloud ear and wood ear), lotus roots & seeds, melons (fuzzy and winter), mung beans, mushrooms, mustard greens, napa cabbage, onions, potatoes, pumpkins, seaweed, taro, tiger lily buds, spinach, sweet potatoes, water chestnuts, watercress

Proteins: Chicken, duck, goose, pigeons, carp, catfish, perch, salmon, shad, trout, armadillos, cranes, deer, hare, partridge, raccoons, roebucks, quail, tortoises, wild ducks, organ meats, beef, lamb, mutton, pork, clams, crabs, fish, lobster, prawns, oysters, scallops, shrimp, squid, cuttle fish, soybean (tofu, dried, fermented, fresh, paste, milk, sauce, sprouts, tempeh, wheat gluten.

Sweeteners: Brown sugar, rock sugar.

Indian Flavors

Grains: barley, corn, millet, rice, sorghum, wheat

Staple Ingredients: Dairy products, fruit, pulses, rice, spices/seasonings, vegetables, wheat.

General flavors: Chiles, coconuts, garlic, ghee, ginger, masalas (dry & paste spice mixtures), onions, saffron, tamarind, turmeric, yogurt.

Condiments & Cooking liquids: Achar (relish/pickles), chutney, coconut oil, mustard oil, raita or pachadi (yogurt condiment), sesame oil, vinegar.

Seasonings: Anise seeds, asafetida, bay leaves, black pepper, cardamom, chiles, cinnamon, cloves, coriander, cumin, curry leaves, fennel seeds, fenugreek, garlic, ginger, mace, mint, mustard (ground & seeds), nutmeg, onion seeds (nigella), pomegranate seeds, dried, poppy seeds, saffron, shallot, tamarind, turmeric.

Fresh, Dried & Pickled: apricots, bananas, betel leaves, cabbage, cauliflower, cherries, coconuts, eggplant, gourds (pitter, bottle, snake, waz), greens (mustard, kale, spinach), jackfruit, lentils (yellow, red, green ,black, brown), limes, mandarin oranges, mangos, melons, okra, onions, papaya, pears, peas, pineapples, pomegranates, potatoes, tamarind, tomatoes, turnips, squash, strawberries.

Proteins: Beans (garbanzo, kidney, mung), eggs, fish and shellfish (mackerel, pomfret, grouper, sole, crab, lobster, mussels, shrimp), beef, buffalo, chicken, goat, lamb, pork, almonds, cashews, pistachios, walnuts, pulses, grains.

Dairy: Buttermilk, cheese (chenna, paneer), cream, ghee, milk, yogurt.

Sweeteners: Fruit (dried and fresh), honey, jaggery (palm sugar).

Japanese Flavors

Grains: barley, corn, rice, wheat, agar-agar (dried red algae), panko (bread crumbs), arrowroot, corn, potato.

Staple ingredients: rice, seafood/seafood products, soybeans, wheat

General Flavor profile: fish stock (dashi), ginger, rice vinegar (yonezu), rice wine (mirin), and sake, sesame, soybean paste (miso), soy sauce, wasabi.

Condiments and Cooking liquids: Chile-bean sauce) toban jiang), pickled ginger (wari), ponzu, rice vinegar, rice wine and sake, sesame oil, soybean paste, soy sauce, teriyaki sauce, tsukemon (pickled vegetables) wasabi.

Seasonings: Black pepper, bonito flakes, dried red chiles, garlic, ginger, mustard, pickled green plums, sansho (similar to ground black pepper), sesame seeds, shichimi togarashi ("seven spice powder"- dried chiles, sansho pepper, poppy seeds, hemp seeds, sesame seeds, dried orange peel, and nori), shiso (perilla)-green and red varieties, sugar, Worcestershire sauce.

Fresh, dried, and pickled: Apples, asparagus, bamboo shoots, bean sprouts, burdock (gobo), carrots, Chinese cabbage (hakusai), citrus fruit- hybrid (yuzu), daikon, eggplant, gourds, grapes, green onions, green plums (ume)- prized for cooking rather than eating raw, greens- mizuna, mitsuba (three leaves), fiddlehead ferns, chrysanthemum greens (shungiku), pepper-tree leaves)- Japanese cucumbers, lotus root, mangos, melons, "mountain vegetables" I.e. spring greens including ferns and ground wort, mushrooms- enoki, shitake, matustake, nameko, shimeji, kikurage-, onions, papaya, passion fruit, pears, persimmons, pineapples, potatoes, snowpeas, squash, sweet peppers, sweet potatoes/yams, taro, turnip- large.

Proteins: Adzuki beans, soybeans, beef, wild boar, chicken, duck, pheasant, fu (gluten cakes), chestnuts, ginko nuts/seeds, sesame seeds, pork, clams, crab, eel, flounder, fugu, katsuo, mackerel, octopus, oysters, red snapper, roe, salmon, sardines, sea urchin, shrimp, trout, tuna, yellowtail.

Korean Flavors:

Grains: barley, corn, rice, sorghum, wheat.
Staple Ingredients: Ginseng, kimchi, rice, soybeans.
General Flavor Profile: Chiles, garlic, ginger, green

onions, sesame, soy.

Condiments and Cooking Liquids: barley malt, hot red pepper paste, rice vinegar, rice wine, sesame oil, soy bean paste, soy sauce.

Seasonings: bean paste, black pepper, chiles, cilantro, cinnamon, citrus (preserved or fermented lemons), garlic, ginger, ginseng, honey, perilla (Japanese basil), sesame oil & seeds, vinegar.

Fresh, dried and pickled: Apples, aralia roots, Asian pear, bamboo shoots, bean sprouts, bellflower root, bracken (fiddlehead fern or fern tip), burdock, carrots, cherries, Chinese cabbage (napa cabbage), crown daisy (chrysanthemum), cucumbers, daikon radishes, eggplant, ginger, gourds, grapes, green onions, jujubes (dried red dates), kimchi, Korean chiles, Korean watercress, leeks, lemons, lettuce, lotus root, melons, mugwort, shitake mushrooms, oak mushrooms, oranges, peaches, peppers, pears, persimmons, plums, potatoes, radishes, spinach, sprouted beans, squash, sweet potatoes, turnips.

Proteins: Soybeans, adzuki beans, mung beans, beef, chicken, chestnuts, gingko nuts, pine nuts, walnuts, pumpkin seeds, sesame seeds, sunflower seeds, pork, abalone, anchovies, algae, clams, cod, cuttlefish, eel, flounder, fluke, herring, mackerel, octopus, pollack, sandfish, sardines, seaweeds, shrimp, squid, tuna, whitefish.

Sweeteners: brown sugar, honey.

Middle Eastern Flavors

Herbs & Spices: allspice, baharat, black pepper, cardamom, carob, cassia, cloves, coriander, cumin, dill, dried fruit, sweet and sour, fenugreek, garlic & garlic chives, ginger, lemon basil, mace, marjoram, mastic, mint, orange water, parsley, poppy seeds, rosemary, rose water, saffron, sesame seeds, sumac, tahini, tamarind, tarragon, turmeric.

Vegetables, fruits, nuts, and legumes: Almonds, black beans chickpeas, eggplant, fava beans, hazelnuts, lemons, lentils, limes (dried, powdered and whole), navy beans, olives, oranges, peppers, pickled vegetables, pine nuts, pomegranate seeds, purslane, red beans, rice, walnuts.

Meat: Lamb.

Dairy: Feta cheese, goat's milk cheese, yogurt (fresh, flavored and dried).

Fats: Butter, olive oil, vegetable oil.

Eastern & Central European Flavors:

Grains: Barley, buckwheat groats, millet, rye, wheat.

Seasonings: Dill, garlic, horseradish, mustard.

Produce: Apples, beets, berries, cabbage, carrots, cucumbers, eggplant, mushrooms, onions, pickled vegetables, potatoes, radishes, sauerkraut, tomatoes, turnips.

Proteins: Beef, chicken, fish (bream, caviar, carp, eel, herring, pike, salmon, sturgeon, trout), lamb, pork.

Dairy Products: Butter, curd cheese (tvorog), cheddar cheese, swiss cheese, feta cheese, kefir, milk, sour cream, cottage cheese, yogurt.

Polish Flavors:

Seasonings: Caraway, cinnamon, cumin, dill, horseradish, juniper berries, marjoram, mustard, paprika, parsley, poppy seeds, vinegar.
Vegetables: Beets, cabbage, mushrooms, onions.
Fruits: Apples, dried fruits.
Meat: Beef, pork.
Dairy: milk, sour cream.

Hungarian Flavors:

Seasonings: Caraway, dill, onions, paprika, parsley, poppy seeds.
Vegetables: cabbage, carrots, cauliflower, cucumbers, kohlrabi, parsley root, peas, peppers, potatoes, sorrel, spinach, tomatoes.
Meat: Beef, game, pork.
Dairy: Milk, sour cream.

Spanish (Spain) Flavors:

Legumes: fava beans, garbanzo beans, kidney beans, lentils, white beans.
Seasonings: Capers, cumin, cured ham, garlic, olive oil

and olives, oregano, paprika, peppers (sweet, hot, fresh, and dry), saffron.

Vegetables: Artichokes and cardoons, asparagus, cabbage, carrots, chard, eggplant, green beans, onions, peas, peppers, potatoes, tomatoes, zucchini.

Fruit: Almonds, apricots, avocados, bananas, carobs, cherimoyas (custard apples), oranges, mandarins, lemons, dates, figs, grapes, wine, raisins, kumquats, mangos, olives, peaches, persimmons, pineapples, plantain, pomegranates, strawberries.

Meat: Beef, lamb, pork, sausages, veal, chickens, rabbits, squab, anchovies, bream, clams, cod, conger eel, hake, mackerel, monkfish, mullet, oysters, prawns, sardines, sea bass, sole, squid, swordfish, trout, tuna, turbot.

Portuguese Flavors

Seasonings: bay leaf, cilantro, cinnamon, cumin, garlic, mint, olive oil, oregano, paprika, parsley, saffron, vinegar, wine.

Produce: Almonds, grapes, lemons, oranges, olives, onions, peppers, potatoes.

Proteins: Bacon, pork, sausage, smoked ham, clams, mackerel, oysters, salt cod.

Northwest France Flavors:

Protein: oysters, lobsters, clams, crabs, skate,

mackerel, lamb, goat, beef, wild boar, rabbit, pheasant, trout, carp, shad.

Dairy: Camembert cheese, cream, butter, goat's milk, sheep's milk.

Produce: apples, plums, pears, potatoes, artichokes, endive, escarole, pumpkins.

Nuts & Grains: Wheat, barley, corn, walnuts.

Northeast France Flavors:

Protein: pork, sausages, terrines, pates, game, foi gras, freshwater fish, escargots, frogs.

Produce: Cherries, grapes, wild mushrooms, potatoes, beets, asparagus, cabbage, sauerkraut.

Cooking fats: Butter, lard.

Dairy: Cow's milk cheese.

Grains: Wheat, spatzle, egg noodles.

Southeast France Flavors

Protein: Beef, pork, lamb, duck, rabbit,

Dairy: cow/sheep/goat's milk cheese,

Produce: apples, grapes, cherries, pears, strawberries, mushrooms, cabbage, potatoes, haricots verts, cardoons, wheat, corn, artichokes, fennel eggplant, tomatoes, peppers, garlic herbs, olives, apricots, cherries, plums, figs (fresh & preserves).

Mediterranean Flavors:

Grains: bulgar, rice, wheat pasta, couscous, unleavened bread, country-style bread, sweet bread.

Legumes: Borlotti beans, cannellini beans, chickpeas, fava beans, lentils.

Nuts & Seeds: almonds, chestnuts, hazelnuts, pine nuts, pistachios, sesame seeds, walnuts.

Herbs: Basil, chives, cilantro, dill, lavender, marjoram, mint, oregano, parsley, rosemary, sage, tarragon, thyme.

Seasonings: Anise seeds, bay leaves, bitter orange peel, black peppercorns, capers, cardamom, chile pepper flakes, cinnamon, cloves, coriander seeds, cumin seeds, fennel seeds, ginger, nutmeg, olives, orange flower water, paprika, preserved lemons, rose water, saffron, sumac, turmeric, zaatar.

Oils: Hazelnut oil, olive oil, walnut oil.

Vinegars: Red and white wine vinegars.

Vegetables: artichokes, arugula, asparagus, broccoli, cabbage, carrots, cauliflower, celery, chiles, cucumbers, curly endive, eggplant, fennel, garlic, leeks, olives, onions, pimientos, potatoes, pumpkins, radicchios, romaine, spinach, sweet peppers, tomatoes, turnips, wild mushrooms, zucchini.

Fruits: Apples, apricots, cherries currants, dates, figs, grapes (wine), lemons, limes, melons, oranges, peaches, pears, persimmons, plums, pomegranates, quinces, raisins, wild strawberries.

Proteins: goat, lamb, pork, rabbit, venison, wild boar, chicken, duck, guinea, quail, rock cornish hens, squab, anchovies, mackerel, monkfish, mullet, sardines, sea bass, tuna, clams, crabs, cuttlefish, mussels, octopus, oysters, rock lobster, shrimp, squid.

Dairy: buffalo mozzarella, feta, sheep & goat cheeses, mascarpone, ricotta, yogurt.

Sweeteners: honey.

Conclusion

I hope you have gained a lot of knowledge from reading this little book. If you bought this book on Amazon, I would appreciate it if you could leave a review. It really helps!

Lastly, I love hearing from readers! If you have questions, comments, or a story to share, please email me:

RenaissanceHousewife@hotmail.com

Thanks for reading, and happy saving!

-Bethany

About the Author

Bethany Bontrager is a happy housewife and caretaker of several goats and chickens. She enjoys reading, writing, farmers markets, homemaking and Scrabble. She and her husband live on five acres in central Michigan.

Bethany blogs about household industry and economy at www.TheRenaissanceHousewife.com.

You can sign up for her monthly email newsletter by going to the "Newsletter & Updates" page at:

www.TheRenaissanceHousewife.com.

More Books by Bethany Bontrager:

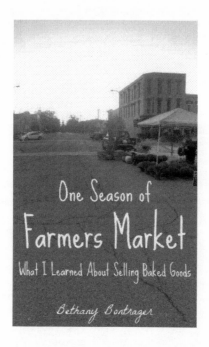

One Season of Farmers Market:

What I Learned About Selling Baked Goods

This book is about what Bethany discovered during her first season
as a farmers market vendor selling baked goods. The first section is
a quick-start guide for aspiring bakers, and the second is Bethany's
own story, told through a series of 21 weekly market updates.

Find out:

- Whether or not you should share your booth (and expenses) with another baker
- What kind of products sell the best and why
- Why people shop at a farmers market anyway
- Whether you should get a booth for the whole season or only certain days
- What role the weather has in your sales
- How sales affect profit
- Emotional ups and downs of being a vendor
- Relating with other vendors
- Relating with customers
- What records to keep and why
- What you should name your business

And much more!

One Season of Farmers Market is available in print or ebook format on Amazon.com.

Pizza Night: A Simple Meal Plan

Are you tired of eating crackers and peanut butter for dinner because there's "nothing to eat" at your house? Are you sick of cooking and washing dishes? Do meal times always sneak up on you, with hungry little people pouncing on you at 5:00 pm? What happens when you run out of peanut butter and crackers?!

You can enjoy meal times again. With a little planning and a little bit of cooking, dinner will NEVER surprise you. Produce will not be rotting in your refrigerator because you forgot to use it. You will lose the weight you gained from only eating crackers, peanut butter, and fast food, and you will probably cut your grocery bill in half.

What have you got to lose? Read this short book and give Pizza Night a try.

Pizza Night includes:

- Meal plans for breakfast, lunch, and dinner, every day of the week
- Variations on almost every meal for variety
- Bonus ideas for snacks and potlucks
- Tips on where to find local food
- Tips to save money on groceries
- Time-saving strategies
- How to personalize the plan for your family

Pizza Night is an ebook available on Amazon.com.

Manufactured by Amazon.ca
Bolton, ON

12669937R00146